It's About Learning
(and It's About Time)

What's in it for schools?

The ability to learn, unlearn and relearn is crucial in a changing and developing world. This book is about understanding the connections between pupils', teachers' and leaders' learning, and between learning in schools and in the wider community. It argues that it is schools' internal capacity that fuels learning, and examines ways that pupils, teachers, parents, school advisors and policy makers can all help increase this capacity to turn schools into learning communities. This fascinating and accessible book contains questions for reflection and inspirational quotes, and should be read by all education practitioners.

Louise Stoll is Professor of Education and Director of the Centre for Educational Leadership, Learning and Change at the University of Bath. **Dean Fink** is an Educational Development Consultant. **Lorna Earl** is an Associate Professor at the Ontario Institute for Studies in Education at the University of Toronto.

What's in it for schools?
Edited by Kate Myers and John MacBeath

Inspection: What's in it for schools?
James Learmonth

Leadership: What's in it for schools?
Thomas J. Sergiovanni

Self-evaluation: What's in it for schools?
John MacBeath and Archie McGlynn

School Improvement: What's in it for schools?
Alma Harris

Assessment: What's in it for schools?
Paul Weeden, Jan Winter and Patricia Broadfoot

It's About Learning (and It's About Time)
Louise Stoll, Dean Fink and Lorna Earl

It's About Learning (and It's About Time)

What's in it for schools?

Louise Stoll, Dean Fink and Lorna Earl

RoutledgeFalmer
Taylor & Francis Group
LONDON AND NEW YORK

First published 2003 by RoutledgeFalmer
11 New Fetter Lane, London EC4P 4EE

Simultaneously published in the USA and Canada by RoutledgeFalmer
29 West 35th Street, New York, NY 10001

Reprinted 2004

RoutledgeFalmer is an imprint of the Taylor & Francis Group

Typeset in Baskerville by
Keystroke, Jacaranda Lodge, Wolverhampton
Printed and bound in Great Britain by
Biddles Ltd, King's Lynn, Norfolk

British Library Cataloguing in Publication Data
A catalogue record for this book is available from the British Library

Library of Congress Cataloguing-in-Publication Data
A catalog record for this book has been requested

ISBN 0–415–22788–7 (hbk)
ISBN 0–415–22789–5 (pbk)

To learners everywhere, especially young learners who are dear to our hearts: Abigail, Zachary, Riley, Christine, Thomas, Alex and Ollie

Contents

Figures

Tables

Series Editors' preface

Kate Myers and John MacBeath

Series introduction

There is a concerted move to raise standards in the public education system. The aim is laudable. Few people would disagree with it. However, there is no clear agreement about what we mean by 'standards'. Do we mean attainment or achievement more broadly defined, for example, and how we are to raise whatever it is we agree needs raising?

At the same time, there appears to be an increasing trend towards approaching changes in education through a controlling, rational and technical framework. This framework tends to concentrate on educational content and delivery and ignores the human-resource perspective and the complexity of how human beings live, work and interact with one another. It overemphasizes linearity and pays insufficient attention to how people respond to change and either support or subvert it.

Recent government initiatives, including the National Curriculum, OFSTED school and LEA inspections, assessment procedures, league tables, target-setting, literacy and numeracy hours, and performance management have endorsed this framework. On occasions this has been less to do with the content of 'reforms' than the process of implementation – that is, doing it 'to' rather than 'with' the teaching profession. Teachers are frequently treated as the problem rather than part of the solution, with the consequence that many feel disillusioned, demoralised and disempowered. Critics of this *top-down* approach are often seen as lacking rigour, complacent about standards, and uninterested in raising achievement.

We wanted to edit this series because we believe that you can be passionate about public education, about raising achievement, about ensuring that all pupils are entitled to the best possible education that society is able to provide – whatever their race, sex or class. We also believe that achieving this is not a simple matter of common sense or of the appliance of science – it is more complex than that. Most of all, we see the teaching profession as an important part of the solution to finding ways through these complexities.

What's in it for schools? is a series that will make educational policy issues relevant to practitioners. Each book in the series focuses on a major educational issue and raises key questions, such as:

* Can inspection be beneficial to schools?
* How can assessment procedures help pupils learn?
* How can school self-evaluation improve teaching and learning?
* What impact does leadership in the school have in the classroom?
* How can school improvement become classroom improvement?

The books are grounded in sound theory, recent research evidence and best practice, and aim to:

* help you to make meaning personally and professionally from knowledge in a given field
* help you to seek out practical applications of an area of knowledge for classrooms and schools ·
* help those of you who want to research the field in greater depth, by providing key sources with accessible summaries and recommendations.

In addition, each chapter ends with a series of questions for reflection or further discussion, enabling schools to use the books as a resource for whole-school staff development.

We hope that the books in this series will show you that there are ways of raising achievement that can take account of how schools grow and develop and how teachers work and interact with one another. *What's in it for schools?* – a great deal, we think!

Acknowledgements

The authors are grateful to the following for permission to reproduce material in this book:

Figure 2.1 from Hyerle, *Visual Tools for Constructing Knowledge*, Alexandria, VA: Association for Supervision and Curriculum Development. Copyright 1996 ASCD. All rights reserved.

Figure 2.2 from Csikszentmihalyi, *Living Well*, Wiedenfeld & Nicholson, 1997.

Figure 4.3 from Dennison and Kirk, *Do, Review, Learn and Apply: A Simple Guide to Experimental Learning*, Blackwell, 1990.

Figure 5.1 from Drake, 'Connecting learning outcomes and integrated curriculum' in *Orbit* 26 (1) (1995): 28–32.

Figure 6.2 from Stoll and Fink, *Changing our Schools*, Open University Press, 1996.

Figure 7.3 from *School Effectiveness and School Improvement*, 10 (4) (1999): 507: figure 1. Copyright Swets and Zeitlinger.

Figure 7.4 from Hill and Crévola, *The Literacy Challenge in Australian Primary Schools*, IARTV Seminar Series No. 69, Melbourne: IARTV, 1997.

Table 3.2 from Johnson *et al.*, *Circles of Learning: Cooperation in the Classroom*, Alexandria, VA: Association for Supervision and Curriculum Development. Copyright 1984 ASCD. All rights reserved.

Table 3.3 from MacBeath *et al.*, *Self-Evaluation in European Schools*, RoutledgeFalmer, 2000.

Table 7.1 from Stoll and Myers, *No Quick Fixes: Perspectives on Schools in Difficulty*, RoutledgeFalmer, 1998.

Lyrics on page 97 from *Everybody Says Don't*, words and music by Stephen Sondheim, copyright 1964, 1973 (renewed) Burthen Music Co Inc, USA, Warner/Chappell Music Ltd, London W6 8BS. Reproduced by permission of International Music Publications Ltd. All rights reserved.

Quote from John Cleese on page 77, reproduced by permission of David Wilkinson Associates.

Excerpt from the poem 'Knots' by R.D. Laing, reproduced by permission of International Thompson Publishing Services.

Letter from *Dear Unknown Friend – Children's Letters from Sarajevo*, New York: Open Society Fund, 1994. Reproduced by permission of the Open Society Institute.

The Poem, *The Door* from *Selected Poems* by Miroslav Holub, translated by Ian Milner and George Theiner, Harmondsworth: Penguin, 1967.

Introduction

In a fast-changing world, if you can't learn, unlearn and relearn, you're lost. Sustainable and continuous learning is a given of the twenty-first century. Why is this? What is learning? Who needs to learn? How can their learning best be enhanced? What is it about schools that appear to be successful at engaging in and sustaining learning? Why is it about time? And what's in it for schools to take what we write seriously? These are the questions we have tried to answer as we connect the need for learning to the reality of the changing world, the increasingly large body of knowledge about what learning is, and the various people in contemporary schools for whom learning is so critical.

There are many books about learning. Some deal with pupils' learning, some with teachers' learning, some with leaders' learning, and some explore organisational learning and learning communities. Few, however, attempt to understand the creation of self-directed and self-motivated learning communities with the capacity to sustain their learning. The ideas usually aren't pulled together into a coherent whole – possibly because it's difficult to do.

What we have attempted to do is to make connections. For this reason we believe that the ideas can be better understood if the book is read from start to finish. We have followed a similar format in most of the chapters, including suggesting 'learnings' for different learners, looking at influences on learners, suggesting how learning of different learners can be enhanced, considering time issues and posing the question 'What's in it for schools?' Each chapter can be read separately but the power and connectedness comes from the whole. That's the message.

In Chapter 1 we provide a rationale for arguing that it's about time there was a focus on learning and that such a focus will mean significant investments of time. In this chapter we attempt to connect learning to the forces affecting the realities of the twenty-first century that make learning for all absolutely essential. Our focus in Chapter 2 is what is known about learning and why learning takes time. We also introduce you to the learners we address in the rest of the book. In Chapter 3 we put pupils (we have chosen the word 'pupils' to refer to pupils and students) where they should be – right at the centre of learning. We ask what it is they need to learn and discuss the difference between learning in young children and adolescents' learning. After exploring the supportive context for pupil learning, we outline ways we believe pupils' learning can be enhanced.

We turn our attention in Chapter 4 to the teacher as learner, considering what teachers need to learn, how adults differ from young learners and what influences teacher learners, before offering ideas for enhancing teacher learning. In Chapter 5 we look at leadership for learning and learning for leadership for learning. After asking what leaders need to learn, we focus on a concept that we have written about before – invitational leadership – to explore how leaders can enhance their own learning as well as creating the conditions for enhancing others' learning. We start linking the learning levels together in Chapter 6 as we explore how the learning community learns together, with members learning from one another. Having outlined what we know about being a learning community and what influences collective learning, we discuss the processes that we believe enhance learning for community.

Finally, in Chapter 7 we argue that schools that are enhancing learning in the ways described in previous chapters are actually enhancing their capacity for sustainable and continuous learning. We pull the ideas from the previous chapters together, identifying nine learning-capacity themes that flow throughout the book. Learning in schools also depends on those outside, so we conclude the book with our own set of 'learnings' for these people so that they can best help enhance the capacity of schools to learn, from outside.

Writing a book like this is a challenge. We have been around long enough, worked with enough schools in many different countries and been involved in enough studies to know that even if you have evidence of 'what works', actually putting it into practice isn't straightforward. Each school has a unique context. So, we aren't providing a recipe to follow – and have done our best to avoid the '100 tips for teachers' that we do not believe promote deep learning or meaningful change. Instead, we pose questions for you to reflect on and offer suggestions and ideas for you to consider and try out, bearing in mind your own individual context. We are trying to cover a huge amount of ground in an accessible way, so that readers can not only refer to it but can use it, we hope, to help them develop capacity for sustainable and continuous learning in their own school(s). We are aware that the knowledge base is fast growing – for example, in brain research – and the world is changing in ways that no one can predict. What we do know is that with a fast-changing world, the evidence that was once valid may no longer be relevant. What's more, to some extent, when you are thinking about futures you are moving into the unknown, and that means that a certain amount of speculation is required.

To help extend the learning process, we have included quotes, examples and tasks for reflection most of which can be done alone but which, in the spirit of the book, we think it would be beneficial to do with colleagues. We have also included an annotated bibliography and website addresses. We haven't attempted to cover the field in this bibliography but have selected books we have found useful and sufficiently user friendly to direct the reader who is interested in exploring ideas further or investigating practical applications.

There are always so many people to acknowledge when writing a book. First, we want to thank Kate Myers and John MacBeath, our series editors, for inviting us to write the book and for their ongoing encouragement. We also greatly appreciate the support and patience of Anna Clarkson, our publisher, and her colleagues at RoutledgeFalmer. Many friends and past and present colleagues have helped shape the ideas in this book. Thanks to those at the University of Bath, OISE/University of Toronto and the Institute of Education, University of London, especially colleagues in CELLC, LEC, ICEC, AGEL and ISEIC (those concerned will know the acronyms!), and our international friends in the International Congress for School Effectiveness and Improvement (ICSEI). We have also shared our evolving ideas with a large number of school leaders and external advisors in England, Canada and several other countries. We are extremely grateful for their feedback and suggestions. Certain individuals have given us feedback on parts of the book, recommended books or quotes, or suggested ideas that we have developed. Thanks to Anne Burrell, Irit Diamant, Sid Freeman, Corrie Giles, Andy Hargreaves, Chris James, Steven Katz, Sarah Litvinoff, Bill Mulford, Yolande Muschamp, Munaza Nausheen, Paul Rangecroft, Jane Reed, Milena Renshaw, Chris Watkins, Felicity Wikeley and Maureen Yeo. We are also extremely grateful to Heather Scott-Duncan for her technical support and endless cheerfulness and to Alex Sing and Lucy Chappel for helping us get the book to the publishers. Finally, our special thanks, as always, go to our families and other loved ones.

Time is a precious commodity (which is one reason we have highlighted it in the title) and when you make the time to read books, you want to feel it has been worth the effort. There are thousands of books out there. What we, and the series editors, are aiming to do is to take a topic that we feel passionate about (and know something, but by no means everything, about) and present the research and ideas accessibly but with the purpose of challenging thinking. We also aim to help readers make connections and come up with creative ideas to promote learning at all levels in their own situations. We hope we have achieved what we set out to do and welcome feedback. As you read the book, you might like to think about this question: If it's not about learning, what should it be about?

1 Why learning?

Where were you when the wall came down? In a sense the Berlin 'wall' fell on each of us. Few people realised as we watched those dramatic pictures on TV of people climbing onto that hated symbol of tyranny and hopelessness, and using chisels, hammers, and any other instrument they could find to destroy it, that all of our lives would change profoundly. Almost overnight the world changed. For the previous 45 years, the interaction of two large power blocs determined the rules of global living. With the disintegration of the eastern bloc and the end of the Cold War, old barriers have broken down to be replaced by integrative globalised structures such as the internet, CNN and McDonalds. This new era is only just over 10 years old – it is in its infancy – yet it is changing by the minute in confusing and unpredictable ways.

As we were putting the finishing touches on this book, the world changed again, starting with the attacks on New York and Washington on 11 September 2001. It is not clear what will follow. There is no doubt, however, that the people of this planet are inextricably connected to one another in the midst of changes that are fast-paced and uncertain.

When we began to think about this book, we started from the premise that to equip future generations to respond and survive in a frenetically and unpredictably changing world, learning was the imperative. Learning has always provided the advantage for human survival through difficult, even seemingly impossible, times. Human beings are able to learn, unlearn, share their learning and pass learning on to those who follow. Learning is at the core of our being, as individuals and collectively. At the same time, our societies have not even approached the limits of what can be learned. As we move into a new century, there are compelling social forces that necessitate better learning and learning in new ways. At the same time, we are on the threshold of major transformations in our learning about learning. The challenge for educators is to apply this new learning to help pupils deal with the opportunities and stresses of shifting and unpredictable social forces on their lives.

In this book, therefore, we attempt:

- to rethink what learning is about, particularly in schools
- to describe what we currently know about learning
- to anticipate what learning might mean for the next generation
- to examine learning in schools (for pupils, for teachers, for leaders, and for schools as learning communities)
- to highlight the links and connections between these levels of learning and what helps promote and sustain them
- to identify learnings for those outside schools to help create the necessary infrastructure to support learning in schools.

The rollercoaster ride of change

Although it is never possible to predict the future, there have been times in human history when people lived with at least the illusion of considerable certainty in their lives. In a rapidly changing world, however, this is no longer possible or even desirable. Educators can't hide their heads in the hope that 'this too shall pass'. They have a choice to make – wait until directed to change by others, or take charge of change and attempt to influence the future of schools and schooling. We concur with Hedley Beare (2001) when he states that it is possible to take 'deliberate actions to maximise the chance of achieving your preferred futures' – for young people, for the teaching profession and for schools.

Possible futures – things which could happen, although many of them are unlikely

Probable futures – things which probably will happen, unless something is done to turn events around

Preferable futures – things that you prefer to have happen and/or what you would like to plan to happen

Beare (2001)

The first step in this process is one of learning: learning about the compelling social forces of our time that influence the course of daily events; learning about the processes of learning; and then building capacity for continuous learning for ourselves and for our pupils. Our 'rollercoaster' of change began in 1989 when the fall of 'the wall' removed international restraints on the forces of globalisation. The ride has only continued to get more thrilling and exciting, but it is also more challenging and frightening.

Globalisation is one of the most talked- and written-about themes in western intellectual circles. It is a very rare political speech or workshop presentation that does not make some reference to globalisation and its promises or threats for the future. Yet, as we have found out as we debated the content and structure of this book, individuals and groups bring very different definitions and perspectives to the concept of globalisation. In very general terms, globalisation is the process by which the peoples and nations of the world are increasingly drawn together into a single entity (Porter, 1999). Facilitated by revolutionary communications technology, globalisation has allowed humans literally to triumph over the limitations of time and space. How one sees the linkages and the implications of this process, however, depends on the lens one uses to view it. For example, globalisation from an economic perspective can be perceived as the spread of free-market capitalism to virtually every country in the world (Friedman, 2000). Looked at from a cultural point of view, globalisation might be perceived as the homogenisation of human culture. As anyone who travels widely will attest, there is considerable evidence that western and particularly American culture are overwhelming and absorbing indigenous cultures. Politically, one might well argue that globalisation is a process of international decision-making that makes national and local governments less important or even impotent. From a third-world perspective one might well view globalisation as 'A new form of colonisation but, instead of being armed with weapons or with Bibles, the new *conquistadors* are bristling with the financial and electronic implements of economic domination' (Mortimore, 2001).

Globalisation is not one process but a complex set of interconnected and interrelated processes that often manifest themselves in contradictory and oppositional ways (Giddens, 1999). To help schools understand the influence of the global forces that have unleashed the powerful forces for educational change buffeting virtually every school and every educator in the western world, we describe five 'forces for change' – economic and work, technological, social, environmental and political.

Economic and work forces

The most obvious manifestation of globalisation is the integration of the world's economies. The idea of a national economy that governments can control and regulate may be a thing of the past. Our economic futures are intricately linked with those of people and nations throughout the world. While globalised economies have always existed, the sheer speed, breadth and facelessness of the ways in which 'the electronic herd' (Friedman, 2000) moves its money, businesses and jobs around the world is unparalleled in human history. This 'herd' is composed of corporations, banks, insurance companies, mutual fund managers and individuals throughout the world who bet on the state of national economies, corporate futures, crop yields and anything else that can be turned to financial advantage. The 'electronic herd' has the potential to require governments internationally to operate under a prescriptive set of principles: reduce the size of government, eliminate national and state debts, cut expenditures on public spending and above all reduce taxes, particularly corporate taxes. Deviations from these rules can result in withdrawal of investment and destabilised economies as has happened, for example, in Malaysia and Mexico. Even labour is subject to the discipline of the electronic herd. Investment goes to the state or nation that can provide stability, profit and fixed and preferably low labour costs (Greider, 1997). Certainly the unionism which has been labour's historical response to exploitation has waned throughout what has been described as 'our global village' (McCluhan, 1964).

These forces have contributed to new patterns of work that are quite different from the past. The idea of a job for life is disappearing. In the late 1990s many young people, when asked how many employers they expected to have throughout their careers, typically responded 'three to five' (Conger, 1997). Entire layers of middle managers have disappeared. More women are working and are increasingly being encouraged by the government in England to do so. Will Hutton (1996) has referred to the 'thirty, thirty, forty society'. He contends that in the United Kingdom, 30 per cent of the adult population is unemployed or employed in government-funded work projects. A second 30 per cent is made up of the 'marginalised and insecure' – people involved in temporary or part-time jobs with few benefits and little future. The final 40 per cent are the 'privileged'; those employed or self-employed adults who have held their jobs for more than two years. Even this group splits into the rich and poor. Thirty-five per cent of the privileged group earns less than 80 per cent of the median wage. For those in work, there is increasing pressure to deliver more quickly and to work harder. Levels of work-related stress are high. In the late 1990s it was estimated that nearly 10 per cent of the UK's GNP was lost each year due to job-generated stress (Arnold *et al.*, 1998), and English researchers have found that beyond 40 hours a week, time spent working is increasingly unproductive and can lead to ill health (Sparks and Cooper, 1997). Newspapers increasingly carry articles about people's desire to 'have a life', high-lighting a 'coming collision' between economic imperatives driving strategies in business and a changing nature of people in the workplace (Bouchikhi and Kimberly, 2000). It is also quite clear that not only will patterns of work continue to change, but the very nature of what we call work will continue to change as a result of technological innovations.

Technological forces

The globalised economy has ridden to power and influence on waves of technological innovation and development that in turn profoundly affect our daily lives. The 'electronic herd', for example, would not exist without a networked society (Castells, 1996).

Technology has improved and enriched our lives in many real and as yet unimaginable ways. There is, however, a cost. The technology that sends people to the moon, cures diseases and facilitates our communication networks also guides smart bombs to their destinations, triggers land mines and supports international terrorism. In the twentieth century technology offered us flight, information technology and medical miracles. It was also a century of sophisticated techno-logical wars, holocausts and anthrax. Technology is value-neutral; it is how we use it that determines its benefits or horrors.

Information technology affects schools directly. There has been an exponential increase in the availability of information, thanks to advanced technologies and particularly the internet. Virtually everyone has access to information once reserved to a small number of experts. One might well argue that, thanks to our advanced information technologies, most people have more information than they are capable of dealing with. Information alone is only useful when it becomes knowledge, unless you are a contestant in a trivia contest. Information becomes knowledge when it is shaped, organised and embedded in some context that has a purpose, that leads one to understand something about the world (Postman, 1999). Different subject disciplines provide intellectual frameworks to help make sense of information and 'turn' it into knowledge. The internet can be a wonderful source of information, but it can also be a repository for the dark side of humankind. A fundamental role for schools is to help pupils use information from the internet critically, to arrive at knowledge that leads to greater understanding. At a higher level, schools play an important role in leading pupils to greater wisdom. To this end, pupils must come to understand which systems of knowledge creation are appropriate for particular problems. In effect, pupils must see the interconnections and interrelationships between and among systems of knowledge creation so that they can make wise and ethical decisions. Just as literacy and media studies involve the critical analysis of literature and the media respectively, these same skills and learning must be brought to existing and emerging technology if we are to attend to the problems of this 'global village'.

> In the Industrial Age, human labor was engaged in the production of goods and the performance of basic services. In the Age of Access, intelligent machines . . . increasingly replace human labor in the agriculture, manufacturing, and service sectors . . . The cheapest workers in the world likely will not be as cheap as the technology coming online to replace them.
>
> Rifkin (2000)

Social forces

According to Phillip Harter, from Stanford University School of Medicine, if the earth's population at the end of the twentieth century could have been shrunk to a village of precisely 100 people, with all the existing human ratios remaining the same, it would have looked something like the following:

57 Asians; 21 Europeans; 14 from the western Hemisphere, both
    north and south; 8 Africans

52 would be female; 48 would be male

70 would be non-white; 30 would be white

70 would be non-Christian; 30 would be Christian

89 would be heterosexual; 11 would be homosexual

6 people would possess 59 per cent of the entire world's wealth and
    all 6 would be from the US

80 would live in substandard housing

70 would be unable to read

50 would suffer from malnutrition

1 would be near death; 1 would be near birth

1 would have a college education

1 would own a computer

Harter (2000)

Harter's village is not static. In 1930 only 33 people lived in the village; at the start of the twenty-first century the population was 100; by the end of this decade it will be 117 people and, at the present rate, 200 people will live in the village by 2050. People are moving, in ever increasing numbers, from the rural parts of the village to the urban sections. In 1950 only 12 people lived in the village's urban environment. By 2005, 50 people will live in this area, and by 2025 the UN projects that 82 people will live in large and small cities in this 'global village'.

As these data suggest, the gap between 'haves' and 'have-nots' in the global village is a chasm, and appears to be growing wider every day as the world's economies become more integrated and globalised. More than a twelfth of the world's population of over six billion live in absolute poverty, including one in six of the world's children. Even within communities such as Britain, the gap between rich and poor continues to widen. A UNICEF report indicates that 20 per cent of young people in Britain live in families below the poverty line (UNICEF, 2000). Ten per cent of children do not have school meals because their parents cannot afford them. Sixty-three per cent of children living in lone-parent families live below the poverty line. The implications of such endemic poverty are staggering. Children in poor households attend school less often, have fewer educational opportunities, have poorer health and have significantly lower achievement than their middle-class counterparts.

Other social changes are occurring. With medical advances, people are living longer, although one newspaper report highlights concerns that our children will have shorter lives than we will, due to less active childhoods and poor nutrition (Norton, 2000). The very notion of family is also shifting from the nuclear family to what David Elkind (1997) calls the permeable family. Permeable families are characterised by many different kinds of kinship relationships, childcare arrangements and practices, and changing attitudes toward childhood. In fact, the very concept of childhood seems to be changing. Childhood is not a biological condition but a social construction. Before the eighteenth century children were considered and treated as little adults. The enlightenment produced the more modern view of childhood as a phase of human development with its own set of needs. There is a growing sense among academics, however, that a more instrumental view of childhood has emerged in recent years. Childhood has become a time to prepare more economically useful adults. Certainly the move away from child-centred learning, and the pressure to test and measure even in early childhood centres, would seem to support this view (Bunting, 2000; Postman, 1999). In many ways, large and small, these changing social forces affect schools. As the one institution that deals with all children, schools have assumed, for better or worse, many responsibilities previously dealt with in the home. Schools now teach children to swim, cook, relate to others, avoid infectious diseases, parent and develop a work ethic. Increasingly schools have also assumed responsibility for helping children and young people to find some meaning in their lives; what Charles Handy would call 'the greater hunger'.

Handy (1997) describes two hungers; 'the lesser hunger' and 'the greater hunger'. 'The lesser hunger' is for the things that sustain life, the goods and services and the money to pay for what we need. 'The greater hunger' is for some understanding of life's purposes. In the global village the pursuit of 'the lesser hunger' has forced an interdependence and interconnectedness among its inhabitants. Paradoxically, the forces that create a more intimate global village have unleashed an equally powerful social force of localisation, and what might be called tribalism (Lasch, 1995) – racial and ethnic particularism – that operates concurrently with globalisation to drive the people of the world apart. Modern communications networks make demands for self-determination and identity of peoples throughout the world possible and realistic. In a world of complexity, instability and unpredictability, people are struggling to make sense of the changes, and to situate themselves within the new milieu. Just as globalisation can destabilise nation states and democratic institutions in the pursuit of profit, tribalism can undermine them in the name of meaning and identity (Barber, 1995).

This 'greater hunger' has motivated large elements of previously marginalised populations, such as women, racial and ethnic groups, the poor and the disabled, to seek more meaningful places in our nations and in the world. It has also contributed to an increase in membership in fundamentalist versions of all the major religions that offer security, predictability and stability in a rapidly changing and somewhat scary world. Taken to extremes, tribalism manifests itself in football hooliganism, holy wars and terrorism. For example, religious and ethnic tensions and clashes have accompanied the disintegration of the Soviet bloc and unleashed patterns of social and cultural collapse and conflict. One need only look at Afghanistan, Bosnia, Chechnya, Kosovo, Macedonia, Turkey, Indonesia, Iraq and Northern Ireland for other examples. This search for meaning finds positive expression in the teaching of indigenous languages, national and regional history and geography, and religious instruction. It can also find negative expression in schools in gangs, cliques and exclusionary schools. On a macro and micro scale in the global village, forces of integration and connectedness confront equally powerful forces of divisiveness and particularism.

> *We hunger to be recognized by others to be cherished for our own sakes and not for what we have accomplished or possess, and to be acknowledged as people who care about something higher and more important than our self interest.*
>
> Lerner (1997)

Environmental forces

Perhaps the one unifier for all of the 'village's' inhabitants is its sustainability as a place for human habitation. Rich or poor, male or female, European or African, we share a village with finite resources.

Forty per cent of the land surface of the village has already been degraded. The increase in the burning of fossil fuels, and the levelling of the village's forests for commercial purposes, as the poorest people try to catch up to the more affluent, have increased the atmospheric concentration of CO_2, and produced a 'greenhouse' effect that alters the 'village's' shorelines and climatic patterns (McCrae, 1995). Nations continue to expend and pollute the village's water sources and alter its entire ecosystem. Most of the population growth in cities comes from its poorest areas. Many of these cities are increasingly becoming 'suppurating sores, without the infrastructure capable of supporting their populations, and producing dysfunctional societies, an inefficient and unequal drain on resources, and some of the world's worst cases of pollution' (Beare, 1996). In Harter's (2000) words, 'When one considers our world from . . . a compressed perspective, the need for acceptance, understanding and education becomes glaringly apparent'. The question now becomes: What kind of education? What do pupils need to learn in order to be 'good' global citizens? The 'village's' survival depends on it.

> Deep ecological awareness recognizes the fundamental interdependence of all phenomena and the fact that, as individuals and societies, we are all embedded in (and ultimately dependent on) the cyclical processes of nature.
>
> Capra (1997)

Political forces

The cumulative impact of these forces has profoundly influenced the political landscape in the global 'village'. Governments internationally deal with the twin pressures of a globalised economy built on the values of the market, competition and efficiency, and increasing demands for social justice and equity on the part of the many who have not benefited from economic and technological changes.

In the absence of international agreement among governments on how to curb the more exploitative aspects of globalisation such as environmental destruction, national governments appear impotent to respond to its abuses. At the same time governments must attend to the concerns of the people who lose out in the globalised world – the homeless, children and the elderly, to mention a few. At the moment, governments at all levels appear to be paring down their historic role and allowing private operators and the market to deal with many functions that were once part of the public service. Political parties and politicians have tended to congregate into four categories based on the twin pressures of how they respond to the globalised marketplace, and how they plan to deal with the social and environmental dislocation it produces (see Figure 1.1). Some believe in the need to actively integrate into the globalised–high-tech society while maintaining a social safety net for those who cannot keep up. Others believe in the integrationist stance but advocate survival of the fittest and if people fall behind 'let them eat cake' (Friedman, 2000). Still others would want to remain separate from the global economy through high tariffs and other devices of economic separatism while supporting those who need help. The final category include those who not only oppose integrating into the global economy, but also would oppose sustaining a social safety net. For the most part, political parties appear to agree on the inevitability of involvement in the globalised economy, but disagree on the degree of government involvement in issues like education, welfare, environmental reform and health care. Where markets have been introduced into the education process, evidence suggests the increased polarisation

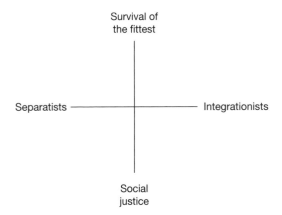

Figure 1.1 Political choices

Source: Adapted from Friedman (2000)

in school intakes leads to a depression of performance in schools with higher proportions of working-class or ethnic-minority pupils with lower prior achievement (Lauder *et al.*, 1999).

Shaped by media owned by gigantic international conglomerates, values have unconsciously been adopted that place consumerism above citizenship, self-interest above public interest and passivity above activism (Saul, 1995). With the exception of countries such as Australia where it is compulsory to vote, fewer than 50 per cent of the electorate vote in many elections. As Saul (1995) describes the situation, civilisations have become unconscious of their need to participate and have lost contact with their responsibilities and their knowledge of the underpinnings of the society in which they live. This paves the way for governments to set the agenda for education. For example, the purpose of education in many countries would seem to be to prepare pupils to make a living, not to prepare them for life. They must therefore do more maths, more science and more computers. If money is needed to finance these areas, then what gets cut are the arts, music and humanities because they are perceived to be of little utilitarian use, even though a number of important learning outcomes can be attributed to arts education (Harland *et al.*, 2000). It is far easier politically to get huge amounts of money to finance accountability processes than to support those things that make us more human.

> The arts are concerned with understanding and expressing the qualities of human experiences. Through music, dance, visual arts, drama and the rest, we try to give form to the feelings and perceptions that move us most as human beings: our experiences of love, grief, belonging, and isolation, and all of the currents of feeling that constitute our experience of ourselves and of others.
>
> NACCCE (1999)

The general political agreement on the need for nations and states to integrate into the global world is, with the exception of splinter groups, part of the political mainstream and a reality that educators must live with. The degree of support for education and particularly state-supported education is, and will continue to be, highly contested politically. Educators who intend to achieve their 'preferred future' must address these issues collectively in the political arena.

Consider each of the following topics: curriculum, teaching, leadership, special education, school organisation. Suggest ways in which the social forces we have described might influence your school(s).

We have asked school leaders in several countries how the forces affect their daily school lives. Many of the impacts are similar; some vary by country or area within country. The three-year election cycle in New Zealand, for example, is seen as exerting particular pressures on educators there.

How do these forces affect your life? Responses from school leaders

Economic and work	Lack of jobs for the unskilled, especially boys. Problems with teacher supply – graduates have greater choice and say 'What's in it for me?' Increasing underclass in poor areas who can't keep up.
Technological	Doesn't always keep pace with the rate of change. Youngsters may know a lot more than adults. Lack of reliability. Lack of access in some cases. Does more lead to better learning?
Social	'We're picking up the pieces of a dysfunctional society.' 'Kids are more open to change.' A greater divide between the haves and have-nots. Greater materialism leading to conflicts of values. Some parents being driven by numbers, others wanting more for their children than just numbers. Staff increasingly facing their own social problems and stress.

Environmental	Disruption of schools from flooding and residue sewage.
	Traffic increase and parents' concerns about the dangers as well as increased pollution and health and sanitation concerns in some areas.
	Greater need to be aware of dangers of over-exposure to the sun.
	Concerns about being expected to be change agents, but just being set up as moral watchdogs when some countries exert pressure for no change to existing environmental policies.
Political	Money coming into schools is attached heavily to strings.
	Increased involvement in curriculum and the ways teachers teach.
	Less freedom to focus on own visions of future learning.

Learning in the twenty-first century

When one looks at the complexity and challenge of the social forces we have identified, a natural question is 'How did we get into this mess?' There are many answers, and too many volumes have been written to synthesise here, but one reason is that traditional ways of knowing would appear not to have made us any wiser. The prevailing intellectual paradigm was shaped 400 years ago. When René Descartes in the late seventeenth century said, 'I think therefore I exist', he set in motion an intellectual revolution that underpins all of our major institutions, especially schools. Reason and rationality became the primary way of knowing. Since he didn't say 'I feel', 'I sense', 'I intuit', 'I remember' or 'I believe', feelings, intuition, memory, ethics and common sense disappeared from intellectual discourse (Saul, 1993).

Newtonian physics proclaimed that we live in an orderly universe that was knowable through rational scientific methods. These notions formed the basis for much of western thought during the past 400 years. Within this intellectual paradigm, the world is knowable through logical, linear, cause–effect techniques. Everything from the universe to the human body can be known and investigated by examining pieces in isolation and looking at the sum of the parts. This kind of reductionism has brought untold scientific and technological triumphs, from the unlocking of the genetic code to the splitting of the atom. It has produced various ways of organising and analysing information into patterns of knowledge. This way of thinking manifests itself in curriculum and pupils being viewed in terms of their parts – the history part, the maths part, the science part and so on.

An alternate view, however, emerges from fields such as quantum physics, molecular biology, Gestalt psychology and ecology. All these disciplines have challenged the conventional rational paradigm. Their proponents have argued that rationality must be balanced by an ecological approach that looks at human and natural systems holistically rather than knowing them through their parts – that we need to examine the interrelationships and interconnections in human and natural systems. For example, the universe is now recognised as chaotic and only knowable through the patterns of relationships and connections among components of the universe (Capra, 1983; 1997). Unlike the mechanical universe of Newton, the universe of the systems-thinker has been likened to a bubbling bowl of porridge, chaotic but producing patterns of activity that are knowable. Within this paradigm, pupils are seen as whole persons who operate in particular contexts and are only knowable and therefore teachable if one is conversant with the patterns that affect the individual's life. Moreover, what they learn can evolve to an even higher level of wisdom. Existing ways of knowing through subjects, for example, help pupils to take random information and structure it in ways that facilitate understanding. Thinking more holistically, however, allows for these various subject approaches to knowledge development to be integrated to help pupils ask questions about their world and understand it in more interconnected ways.

We share the beliefs of the International Commission on Education for the Twenty-first century who wrote a report to UNESCO, inspiringly titled *Learning: The Treasure Within*. In it, Jacques Delors and his co-authors (1996) argue that:

traditional responses to the demand for education that are essentially quantitative and knowledge-based are no longer appropriate. It is not enough to supply each child with a store of knowledge to be drawn on from then on. Each individual must be equipped to seize learning opportunities throughout life, to broaden her or his knowledge, skills and attitudes, and to adapt to a changing, complex and interdependent world.

To this end, the Commission proposes 'four fundamental types of learning which, throughout a person's life, will in a way be the pillars of knowledge':

- *Learning to know* – acquiring a broad general knowledge, intellectual curiosity, the instruments of understanding, independence of judgement, and the impetus and foundation for being able to continue learning throughout life.
- *Learning to do* – the competence to put what one has learned into practice, even when it is unclear how future work will evolve, to deal with many situations and to act creatively on one's environment. This involves higher skills at all levels, being able to process information and communicate with others.
- *Learning to live together* – developing understanding of and respect for other people, their cultures and spiritual values, empathy for others' points of view, understanding diversity and similarities between people, appreciating interdependence, and being able to dialogue and debate, in order to participate and co-operate with others, enhance relationships, and combat violence and conflict.
- *Learning to be* – developing the 'all-round' person who possesses greater autonomy, judgement and personal responsibility, through attending to all aspects of a person's potential – mind and body, intelligence, sensitivity, aesthetic sense and spiritual values – such that they can understand themselves and their world, and solve their own problems.

As the UNESCO authors and others have argued, formal education has generally concentrated on the first two, leaving the others to chance, or assuming that they will result from the other two. Constantly shifting global forces, however, will have an impact not only on what we need to learn but also on our thinking about the very role of learning and will make *learning to live together* and *learning to be* as basic as *learning to know* and *learning to do*.

In a survey of experts in nine eastern and western countries, there is consensus on eight necessary characteristics of twenty-first century citizens if they are to cope and constructively engage with these global changes (Cogan and Derricott, 2000). They are: looking at problems in a global context; working co-operatively and responsibly; accepting cultural differences; thinking in a critical and systemic way; solving conflicts non-violently; changing lifestyles to protect the environment; defending human rights; and participating in politics. As we have completed writing this book, many of these characteristics have taken on greater poignancy and urgency given the events in America on 11 September 2001 and international soul-searching about appropriate responses.

Consider each global force. What will pupils need to learn to know, to do, to be and to get along with others in order to deal with economic, technological, social, environmental and political forces?

The reforms of recent years have focused largely on standards and structures. These are important – standards especially; but they have almost nothing to say about whether the system can help students become capable of meeting the more complex demands that will be made on them in the future.

Bayliss (1999)

. . . And it's about time

The *double entendre* about time in our title shows the importance that we attach to it. Not only do we think that 'it's about time' for the agenda of educational reform to be focused on learning as the fundamental purpose of schools; it is also about the time that teachers, heads and other educational professionals will need to refocus schools on learning. It's about recognising different conceptions of time and the pace of change that adults and children are experiencing in education world-wide. Everything around us is speeding up. Changes in education are no exception – they are occurring at an unprecedented pace and many people that we talk to in schools are feeling stressed and overwhelmed (Hargreaves *et al.*, 2000). These are certainly not the ingredients for the kind of educational revolution that the focus on learning requires. Throughout this book, therefore, we will attempt to suggest practical ways of attending to issues of time.

Time to reorient the agenda

In the 1980s Tom Peters and Robert Waterman exhorted business people to 'stick to their knitting': in other words, attend to their core business. We have already argued that our knitting is and should be learning, and yet the public discussions of education might lead one to believe that the knitting is 'achieving targets', 'doing well on the league tables', 'getting through OFSTED', 'getting good SATs or GCSE results', or 'being an oversubscribed school'. While we believe that pupil achievement is extremely important, we would suggest that such a narrow focus is misguided. Somewhere along the way, in the name of educational reform, policy makers may have confused structure with purpose, measurement with accomplishment, means with ends, compliance with commitment, and teaching with learning. In an attempt to reposition education for a post-modern world of diversity, complexity, uncertainty and innovation, governments around the world seem determined to 'polish yesterday's [educational] paradigm' (Peters, 1999). We propose a bolder stance. Innovation requires creativity, imagination, autonomy and risk taking. To respond to these needs, an educational system must possess the same characteristics. We argue, therefore, that the agenda for reform must be redirected towards the essential purpose of education: learning – learning to create, solve problems, think critically, unlearn and relearn, and to care about others and the environment.

Time for genuine learning

One of the challenges we face is that people's conceptions and experiences of time differ. Larry Cuban (1995) has described five clocks of school reform that operate on a different time zone and are viewed from different perspectives:

- *Media time* is the fastest reform clock that ticks every second of every day, like a video on fast forward.
- *Policymaker time*, Cuban claims, chimes every two to four years (we think it is more often!), producing new policies and programmes that may be more sensitive to public sentiment than to the reality of life in schools.
- *Bureaucratic time* chimes when new rules are announced, with a lag between this and policy time.
- *Practitioner time* is slower and grows over decades – as Michael Fullan (2001) has reminded us, 'Change is a process not an event'.
- *Pupil learning time*: here the lag between clocks is even greater, and this clock is the hardest to read because it is difficult to separate from home-based and other learning that takes place outside school. It may show up years after formal schooling has ended, since children's speed and style of learning varies.

Perhaps more attention to practitioner and pupil learning clocks would shift the public debate further towards the substantial matters of classroom learning and teaching and, importantly, towards real innovation. Of course there is a paradox here because, while it takes time for teachers to learn and embed new practices, for the pupils it's the only time they have. Their school years are precious ones and can't be repeated. This means that there really is a sense of urgency.

List examples of how each of the clocks operate in your context.

Since turbulent conditions appear everywhere and pervade our lives in both time and space, learning in permanent white water conditions is and will continue to be a constant way of life for all of us – thus the phrase learning as a way of being.

Vaill (1996)

What's in it for schools?

Schools are part of 'nested systems'. They are 'nested' in their communities, Local Education Authorities (LEAs), geographic areas, counties, provinces or states, nations, regional economic and political associations like the European Union, and the international family of nations. Knowledge of how each layer affects our schools is vital to our ability as educators to determine what our pupils need *to know, to do* and *to be* and how and why they must learn *to live together*. It is also important for teachers and school leaders who are responsible for the implementation of government policies to understand the social forces that shape the thinking of policy makers and the course of events in schools (Fink, 2001). Through the constant scanning of these layered environments, we as educators can design the learning experiences that will help our pupils to function in rapidly changing contexts. Fortunately for us, the past 20 years have yielded a great deal of learning about how people learn. The challenge for educators, then, is to learn how to change in order to help our pupils to learn to deal with change. In the next chapter we develop these ideas by focusing on what we now know about learning.

> Identify paradoxes, ironies and oxymorons related to your educational context. What issues do they raise for the improvement of learning?

Further readings

Thomas Friedman's *The Lexus and the Olive Tree* provides an economic perspective on globalisation for the non-economist.

In *The State We're In* Will Hutton, now Chief Executive of the Work Foundation, describes the impact of globalisation in Britain and differing ideological responses.

Capitalism and Social Progress, by Phillip Brown and Hugh Lauder, provides a comprehensive and readable analysis of the social forces that are driving changes in the world. For educators, they connect these forces to the world of education in ways that help the reader to answer the question, Why do schools have to change? Their concept of 'collective intelligence' provides a healthy alternative to contemporary policy directions.

Stephen Sterling offers a clear, concise and passionate argument for taking a holistic, ecological orientation to education in *Sustainable Education: Revisioning Learning and Change*. He suggests a new educational paradigm that can help sustain the 'whole person', communities and the environment. See also www.schumacher.org.uk

Jeremy Rifkin's *The Age of Access* argues that the market has changed and that the sale of goods and services has been replaced by temporary, long-term leasing arrangements. Ownership is a thing of the past. The key to economic prosperity will be access to the 'net'.

The work of Fritjof Capra develops the ideas of shifting intellectual paradigms in great detail and outlines their significance for the sustainability of our planet. The most accessible of his works are *The Web of Life* and *The Turning Point*.

In *Taking Education Really Seriously*, Michael Fielding has skilfully brought together a number of writers who offer a range of perspectives on the New Labour government's performance over its first four years. It's a serious read, with some insightful contributions.

John Ralston Saul develops an engaging and challenging perspective on societal changes. He suggests that modern societies are captives of reason and rationalism and have allowed faceless technocrats to seize power. While somewhat difficult going, *Voltaire's Bastards* can generate serious intellectual debate and challenge conventional wisdom. *The Unconscious Civilization* is a more accessible volume.

Tomorrow's Citizens, edited by Nick Pearce and Joe Hallgarten, resulted from a conference on citizenship held by the Institute for Public Policy Research (IPPR). As the editors highlight, beneath the consensus supporting the value of citizenship education lie major and vital questions about its definition, purposes and intended outcomes. (The book is available through Central Books.)

2 Learning about learning

Throughout history people have wondered about learning. What is it? How does it happen? How is human learning different from animal learning? Needless to say, there are no simple answers. Many academics (from psychologists to neurophysiologists) are still working to understand how the mind works and how people learn. We may not have absolute answers but there have been extraordinary advances in the past few decades. Certainly, as David Perkins commented almost a decade ago, we know enough to do a much better job of education by drawing on current knowledge of how learning works and how to motivate learning.

> *We do not have a knowledge gap about learning, we have a* monumental *use-of-knowledge gap.*
>
> *Perkins (1992)*

What have we learned about learning? First, no one has yet been successful in developing a single comprehensive theory of learning that covers all of the kinds of learning that we do, although many great minds since the time of Plato have tried. Instead, we have to be content to deal with a number of theories, each useful in its own way. There are many different types of learning, some simple and some complex; some involve the acquisition of knowledge and others the mastery of skills; some can be learned from experience and some need to be taught. For Plato, learning was innate. Descartes brought us the notion of rational, deductive reasoning as a way of analysis and organisation to expose the 'true nature of things'. Locke saw the mind as 'tabula rasa' – a blank slate waiting to be filled; and Skinner identified the power of reinforcement in learning. One common element in these theories was the belief that learning was something that *happened to* the learner.

In the last century, however, there have been huge advances in our understanding of how learning occurs. Psychologists have introduced the notion of the mind as an active, malleable living thing that grows and adapts in response to the environment. Piaget's (1980) theory placed action and self-directed problem solving at the heart and highlighted specific universal stages in development associated with cognitive functioning. Vygotsky (1962) theorised that human learning is dependent on the social and cultural environment, as well as the mind, and that the deep determinants of human activity lie in the historically developing culture, embodied in various signs and symbol systems. This parallels Bruner and Haste's (1987) description of learning as 'interweaving' language, interaction and cognition. As John Dewey described it early in the twentieth century, thinking happens when a person experiences a problem understanding something. The mind actively jumps back and forth – struggling to find a clearer formulation of the problem, looking for suggestions, for possible solutions, surveying elements in the situation that may be relevant, drawing on prior knowledge and cultural beliefs in an attempt to understand the situation. The mind eventually begins forming a hypothesis about how best the problem might be understood and/or solved. The hypothesis is then tested in the larger cultural context and either the solution holds or the search goes on.

Take, for example, the following situation. A five-year-old niece approached one of us and announced that 'all cats are girls and all dogs are boys'. When asked why she believed this to be true, she responded: 'Our cat is a girl and she's little and smooth, girls are little and smooth, too. The dog next door is a boy and he's big and rough, just like boys are big and rough. Cats are girls and dogs are boys.' This interchange showed that she was struggling with a problem, she surveyed her environment, gathered data, formulated a hypothesis and, when she tested it, it held. This is pretty sophisticated logic. When she was shown a picture of a chihuahua, a dog that was little and smooth, and asked about its gender she said: 'It's a boy, . . . sometimes they can be little and smooth'. But, when confronted with a picture of an Irish setter with all her puppies, she was perturbed. After a last hold-out comment, 'Maybe it's the dad', she asked: 'Can dogs be girls?'

This anecdote shows the complexity of the learning process, as the learner connected what she believed to be true with new information and tested her understanding in her social context. Learning is not passive and brains are not receptacles waiting to be filled with information. Learning is an active, dynamic process that requires effort and energy that is both individual and social. This conception of learning challenges much of the widely held 'folk psychology' of development and learning. However, it is the key to making significant progress in education.

> Observe a learner closely. Listen to what she/he says. Watch what she/he does. What does this tell you about the process of learning in this case?

What do we know about learning?

Learning is intellectual, social and emotional. It is linear and erratic. It happens by design and by chance. We all do it and we take it for granted, even though we do not have a clear understanding of what it means or how to make the most of it. Schools operate with a multiplicity of conceptions of the nature of learning, from knowledge as the *stuff* to fill pupils' waiting minds, to a view suggesting that there is no reality beyond that which is constructed in the language of the members of a society. In the rest of this chapter, we describe some of what is currently known about the learning process, in order to reinforce not only its complexity but also the importance of understanding why learning about learning matters.

Learning is making connections

The past 50 years of research have made it clear that learning is not a passive process. Young minds don't come empty of ideas ready to receive our wisdom any more than adult minds are sponges absorbing new ideas from the air. From the earliest days, the minds of infants are active and toiling to make sense of the world around them. Over time, this sense-making activity is made up of conscious attention, organising and reorganising ideas, assimilating or accommodating to new ideas, and constant reshuffling and reorganising in efforts to connect ideas into coherent patterns.

For learning to occur, there must be some level of *consciousness* – that combination of biological architecture and self-directed action allowing one to perceive and think about what is happening outside and inside oneself in such a way that it can be evaluated and acted on (Csikszentmihalyi, 1990). Outside events don't exist for people unless they are aware of them. Consciousness screens what is perceived by the senses, actively shaping events and imposing a personal understanding on them. Very simply, information enters consciousness when someone focuses attention on it or because something about it commands attention.

Attention is like psychic energy that can be controlled in order to engage in other mental events like remembering, thinking, feeling and ultimately learning. Once something enters consciousness, the human mind goes to work to organise it and connect it to what it already knows. This involves processing the information, searching for and retrieving information from memory or experience, checking the match between the new information and prior knowledge, monitoring comprehension, reorganising ideas and coming to decisions about what the new information means and where it fits. All of this activity happens at lightning speed; generally the learner is completely unaware of the process.

When the new information is largely consistent with prior ideas and beliefs, it is usually combined easily with existing knowledge and reinforces the existing views. This is referred to as *assimilation* (Posner *et al.*, 1982). On the other hand, if the new information is inconsistent or in conflict with existing ideas, the learner may be required to transform his/her beliefs and the process is called *accommodation* (Posner *et al.*, 1982). Accommodation is much harder than assimilation. It creates dissonance and disorder, and it requires sustained attention and energy. This is not just a cognitive process; it is emotional, as we shall show later, because every piece of information gets evaluated for its bearing on the self and the potential effect on the learner's environment. Even though accommodation is hard, it is also essential for conceptual change and, therefore, serious learning. Learning results from these episodes of dissonance (Linn and Songer, 1991; Olsen and Bruner, 1997), just as it did in the cat and dog story.

> New insights don't happen by osmosis. They come from facing ideas that challenge the familiar ways of viewing issues.
>
> Earl and Katz (2002)

For many people, learning feels like a random activity. It just happens (or it doesn't). Unless a person knows how to order his or her thoughts, attention goes to whatever is in the immediate environment and the learner will often wallow in the psychic entropy of confusion and uncertainty. But learning is something that can be controlled and enhanced by focusing attempts to make sense of information, to relate it to prior knowledge, and master the skills involved. This process occurs when someone monitors what is being learned and uses the feedback from this monitoring to make adjustments, adaptations and even major changes in what is understood.

Achieving an ordered state of mind is not an easy task. Somehow the wealth of information existing outside a person becomes part of an individual's internal 'knowing'. Ideas provide the base for learning and educate attention so that one can access the rich knowledge base in the environment. Costa (1996) has identified nine uniquely human strategies for harnessing information and making sense of the world through an intentional process of learning (see Figure 2.1).

- *Metacognition*: Human beings can reflect on their own thinking processes. Experts describe their thinking as an internal conversation – monitoring their own understanding, predicting their performance, deciding what else they need to know, organising and reorganising ideas, checking for consistency between different pieces of information and drawing analogies that help them advance their understanding.
- *Constructing abstraction*: Humans have the capacity to use language, images and numbers as symbols to transform events into categories and patterns. These symbolic systems make it possible for people to think in abstractions and to order and reorder the world in thought.
- *Storing information outside the body*: Humans store, organise and retrieve information in and from locations other than their bodies. From cave drawings, to books, to videodisks, external storage and retrieval systems provide access to information far beyond the limits of memory.

Figure 2.1 What makes humans human?

Source: Costa (1996)

- *Systems thinking*: Humans are able to see patterns, congruencies and inconsistencies while still focusing on the whole. This capacity allows them to consider many perspectives and to imagine how changing one element can have an impact on the total system.
- *Problem finding*: Not only are humans able to search for problems to solve; they appear to enjoy it. Humans question and sense ambiguities and anomalies in the world around them. Once there is some doubt, they look for better ways of understanding the nature of things.
- *Reciprocal learning*: Human beings are social creatures with a compulsive craving to engage with each other. They learn best in groups, as they listen to one another, strive for agreement and rethink their beliefs and understanding.
- *Inventing*: Human beings are creative and are often motivated intrinsically, rather than extrinsically, to work on tasks because of the challenge. They constantly strive for greater fluency, elaboration,

novelty, parsimony, simplicity, craftsmanship, perfection, harmony, beauty and balance.

- *Deriving meaning from experience*: One of the most significant attributes of human beings is that they can reflect on and learn from their experiences. They can stand back, monitor activities and modify actions or beliefs.
- *Altering response patterns*: Although a certain amount of human activity may be hard-wired, people are able to make significant conscious and deliberate choices about their behaviour. They are always capable of learning and altering their responses based on new ideas or understanding.

Costa's framework accentuates the view that learning is not a static trait; learning is a dynamic process that itself can be learned and developed. Humans have many different ways of approaching something new, of investigating it and of making sense of it. Viewed this way, learning is an ongoing, iterative process of fitting information into patterns or schema of similarities, differences, likenesses and regularities. As learning progresses, learners move beyond the basic rules associated with any field until it becomes automatic and they are comfortable in a domain and begin to build their own understanding by acting, assessing what happens, reflecting, designing new strategies and acting again.

The human mind operates by constructing something like a mental model, an internal representation allowing the individual to retrieve information efficiently and use it by making connections to other ideas. Each one of us makes up a story based on prior knowledge, experiences and teaching. If the wrong mental connections are made, the learner can get very lost. Just like trying to negotiate a new town with inaccurate or limited maps, it is hard to follow directions or reach a destination without good mental maps. These mental maps are constructed through both physiological connections and logical organisers. The next sections address these issues.

Learning is a constructive process that occurs best when what is being learned is relevant and meaningful to the learner and when the learner is actively engaged in creating his or her own knowledge and understanding by connecting what is being learned with prior knowledge and experience.

Lambert and McCombs (1998)

Learning and its relationship with the brain

One of the most significant advances in understanding learning has come from neuroscience. Without the ability to see inside the brain, beliefs about the nature of learning have been based on inferences drawn from logic and from behaviour – the domains of philosophers and psychologists. With the advent of brain-imaging technologies, such as PET scans, and genetic research, scientists are beginning to be able to watch minds at work and the conceptions of how learning happens are being altered radically. In simple terms, it appears that the brain is a living organism that grows and reshapes itself as it develops and is used. In essence, we make our brains as we use them. The brain that eventually takes shape is the result of interactions between the individual's genetic inheritance and everything the person experiences. As Wolfe and Brandt (1998) describe it:

> Children are born with a kind of biological "power pack" of social and intellectual predispositions. Predispositions are best described as encoded sets of processes, ways of thinking and doing things which . . . represent a set of inherited appropriate practices that are transmitted from generation to generation. Whether or not these are used within a particular generation depends entirely on environmental challenges and other intrinsic motivations.

At birth, the brain already has all of the neurons it will ever have. The early years are the peak learning years, as neural connections form rapidly and the brain adapts and reorganises itself into layers of interconnecting neural networks. It appears to develop some capacities at critical periods in the early years. Predispositions open up at points in development and, if these predispositions are not used, that section of the brain gets used for something else. In one research study, Marion Diamond (1988) established that the brains of adult rats also form new synapses in response to complex environments. Susan Greenfield (1997) maintains, however, that caution is needed about social implications of this kind of research. It is not the enriched environment, *per se*, that is important, but the challenge of such an environment leading to stimulation of the brain. Adult brains, therefore, remain highly plastic and capable of extensive neural reorganisation throughout life, and

Greenfield reassuringly states that although older people perform worse on certain problem-solving tasks and are a little slower in processing information, there is no evidence that learning decreases with age. To use her words, 'Old age can be the ultimate expression of you as an individual'.

Learning and understanding

There is a great deal of talk these days about 'learning for deep understanding'. But just what does 'learning for understanding' mean? What is deep understanding? Brandsford and colleagues (1999) provide an example using Einstein's theory of relativity. What would constitute evidence that someone understood $E=MC^2$? Reciting the equation only shows that it has been remembered; it does not show that it has been understood. Understanding involves knowledge about energy, mass, velocity of light and mathematical notions like 'square'. But this isn't enough. One would have to be able to use these concepts according to rules of physics, to support the theory with evidence, to identify the problems the theory solves and the theories it replaces, and so on. Deep understanding is having a grasp of the structure of a discipline, seeing how things are related, using the ideas in novel situations and evaluating, even challenging, the knowledge claims embedded in the discipline.

Understanding is knowledge in thoughtful action.
Perkins and Unger (2000)

Thinking and learning depend on having a rich base of knowledge about the subjects under consideration and a great deal of experience to become comfortable with the ideas and create the mental maps that organise them. Prior knowledge of a topic or idea provides the foundation for linking new ideas and building complex mental maps but as the Einstein example shows, knowledge in itself doesn't guarantee understanding. Studies that examine differences between experts and novices have provided enormous insights into how knowledge and understanding work together (Brandsford *et al.*, 1999). Novices may lack important knowledge or have memorised a wealth of disconnected facts, without any organising structure or concept to provide understanding or transfer to new situations. In the early stages of learning something, learners need rules to help them see the order of things and develop their own knowledge and schema for future reference. After time, they become sufficiently proficient that they can move outside rigorous adherence to the rules.

> The research ... shows clearly that 'usable knowledge' is not the same as a mere list of disconnected facts. Experts' knowledge is connected and organized around important concepts (e.g., Newton's second law of motion); it is 'conditionalized' to specify the contexts in which it is applicable; it supports understanding and transfer (to other contexts) rather than only the ability to remember.
>
> Brandsford *et al.* (1999)

Experts organise and classify their knowledge around important concepts and draw on these configurations of 'usable knowledge' in their thinking because the ideas have become automatic parts of their thinking. With this kind of automaticity, experts can use the concepts in an unstructured world where there are very complex interactions of multiple factors. They take personal responsibility for the outcomes of their learning work; they fine-tune their understanding by checking it against other information; and they use self-monitoring to signal the need for a return to the rules or a search for new information.

> There is something I don't know
>   That I am supposed to know.
> I don't know *what* it is I don't know
>   and yet I'm supposed to know,
> And I feel I look stupid
> If I seem both not to know it
>   and not know what it is I don't know.
> Therefore, I pretend I know it.
>   This is nerve-racking
>   since I don't know what I must pretend to know.
> Therefore, I pretend to know everything.
>
> (excerpt from 'Knots' by R. D. Laing)

One of the obstacles to this process flowing smoothly is that people often don't know what they don't know. The world that they have constructed is coherent and makes sense to them. There doesn't seem to be any need to move beyond. Dubin (cited in Watkins *et al.*, 2000) offers a useful matrix of various states of a learner in relation to their recognised need to learn something, suggesting that 'conscious incompetence' is the ideal state at the start of learning (see Table 2.1).

We noted earlier that learning means reinforcing, creating new, or challenging existing mental organisational structures. Learning is a continuous process of both assimilation (addition of new mental maps) and accommodation (modification or change of existing mental maps). Arguably the most difficult of these processes occurs when an individual faces challenges to their view of the world. It will come as no surprise that human beings are very adept at avoiding or ignoring new ideas or ideas that don't fit easily into their view of the world. Nowhere is this dissonance more obvious than when existing beliefs and convictions about 'what is' are challenged or even debunked. Throughout history, the human race has had to make significant conceptual changes as new knowledge emerged. Examples include how our ancestors adjusted to notions of a round planet rather than a flat earth; of an earth that circled the sun and was not the centre of the universe; and of germs, not evil spirits, as the cause of disease. In recent times we have seen many other examples, such as mapping of the human genome. The dramatic changes we described in Chapter 1 require people to confront radical differences between what is emerging and their personal beliefs or knowledge. There was a time when very little changed during any generation. Now, radical

Table 2.1 Four possible states of the learner

	Unconscious of need to learn a specific skill or knowledge	**Conscious** of need to learn a specific skill or knowledge
Incompetent in relation to a specific skill or knowledge	**Unconscious incompetence**	**Conscious incompetence**
Competent in relation to a specific skill or knowledge	**Unconscious competence**	**Conscious competence**

Source: Dubin (cited in Watkins *et al.*, 2000)

changes in society's understanding of a whole range of phenomena take place in any generation, maybe more than once. More and more sophisticated learning, then, is not just a

> ... *our ability to thrive depends on our capacity to learn.*
> *Bentley (2000)*

nice idea. It is a necessity for human survival and adaptation.

At the same time, learning is hard work – especially learning for understanding that requires retention, organising principles and the active use of knowledge. This is 'deep learning', as distinct from 'surface learning' (Marton, 1975), where tasks are seen as unrelated and there is an emphasis on memorising, accompanied by an unreflective attitude. Deep learning is far more likely to embody serious personal commitment to learning (Askew and Carnell, 1998). This leads us to the critical issue of motivation.

Learning and motivation

If learning is such hard work and requires focused attention, it should come as no surprise that people are not always eager and ready to learn. We have noted that learning happens in the dissonance that occurs when ideas are put forward for questioning, examination and possibly for radical changes. At the same time, people tend to strive for relative stability between their internal conceptions and new information. The challenge for learners is to move beyond dissonance into productive learning. But what is it that compels people to live in the dissonance, experience the discomfort of not understanding something, and strive to integrate new knowledge, even when it requires serious adjustments to their prior beliefs? What motivates learning? Perhaps the most compelling answer resides in the simple question, 'Why?' For pupils, 'Why are we studying this?' For teachers, 'Why should I change my practices?' For leaders, 'How will the organisation benefit?' And perhaps most compelling for all of them, 'What's in it for me?'

If humans are inherently drawn towards making sense of their surroundings (and this curiosity is particularly strong for young children), understanding how motivation works provides the key to keeping learning at the forefront and building patterns of learning that are automatic and last a lifetime. From a very early age, children develop theories about how the mind works and what it means to learn. These beliefs are often very powerful and can have a profound influence on how they situate themselves in relation to learning. Researchers have discovered that there are dramatic cultural differences in the way teachers, pupils and students view the relative importance of ability and effort in their success.

> The relative emphasis given to ability and effort has direct implications for the way people think about learning. In American society, learning tends to be regarded as an all-or-none process. A student who is 'bright' is expected to just 'get it', whereas duller students are assumed to lack the requisite ability for ever learning certain material. Under the 'ability' model, motivation to try hard depends a great deal on the individual child's assessment of whether s(he) has the ability to succeed. By contrast, the effort model, such as the Chinese and Japanese tend to hold, portrays learning as gradual and incremental, something that almost by definition must be acquired over a long period of time.
>
> (Stevenson and Stigler, 1992)

Does your school/workplace promote a learning orientation or performance orientation (see Table 2.2)?

Table 2.2 Different motivational styles and their characteristics

Performance orientation	Learning orientation
Belief that ability leads to success	Belief that effort leads to success
Concern to be judged as able and to perform	Belief in one's ability to improve and learn
Satisfaction from doing better than others or succeeding with little effort	Preference for challenging tasks
Emphasis on interpersonal competition and public evaluation	Derives satisfaction from personal success at difficult tasks
Helplessness: evaluates self negatively when task is difficult	Applies problem-solving and self-instruction when engaged in tasks

Source: Based on Dweck (1986)

The extent to which individuals see themselves as competent and capable has a dramatic effect on their willingness to attempt new learning. People consciously or unconsciously ask questions like: 'How uncomfortable will it make me?' 'For how long?' When people consistently fail, they lose their motivation to learn and go to great lengths to avoid the pain of failure, the possibility of public humiliation and additional confirmation of their incompetence. In essence, human beings deal with threat by down-shifting, turning off and resisting engagement.

Motivation also flags when someone succeeds too easily. There is no reason to continue to expend energy. Csikszentmihalyi (1990) explains that if a person has few skills and faces little challenge, they are apathetic, while if challenge is low but their skill level is higher, they are likely to experience boredom. When both levels of challenge and skill are high, they are in 'flow' (see Figure 2.2).

When people believe they are able to succeed, they are willing to try new and challenging tasks, even when they are difficult. Continuous

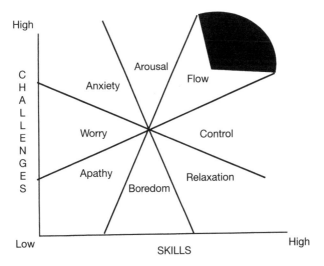

Figure 2.2 Flow: optimal experience

Source: Csikszentmihalyi (1997)

learning therefore appears to depend on a combination of hard work and obvious success.

For a long time, reinforcement and rewards have been considered as important motivators. When initial interest in a task is low, rewards can increase the likelihood of academic engagement and performance of tasks. However, there is a paradox about the nature and power of rewards when the task is intrinsically interesting. Extrinsic rewards have the potential to undermine performance, especially with tasks that people are likely to do in the absence of any reward because they are inherently interested. There is a danger that when people who are highly intrinsically motivated are faced with a heavy accountability system of extrinsic rewards, they lose some of the intrinsic motivation and replace it with reinforcement from the reward. It is then very hard to return to intrinsically motivated behaviour.

Four broad categories of motivation:

Extrinsic	central to surface learning, the task is carried out because of positive or negative reinforcing consequences
Social	relating to the influence of the person who formed the motive (parent, peer or teacher) and the nature of the process (modelling, conformity or co-operation)
Achievement	learning for the purpose of passing a test or getting a job, this is surface motivation, exemplified in actions such as rote which may, nonetheless, produce academic success
Intrinsic	deep learning for its own sake, with personal commitment

Biggs and Moore (1993)

Learning is emotional

Learning is not the exclusive purview of the intellect. It is also deeply emotional. The emotions of learning are often overlooked; nevertheless, buried not too far below the neocortex or thinking parts of the brain lie the brainstem and the limbic system that are responsible for the emotional system. The brain circuitry that connects these different parts of the brain allows for the subtlety and complexity of human emotions. As Goleman (1996) describes in his book *Emotional Intelligence*, thinking and rationality are the engine of our choices but feelings and emotional intelligence help to streamline decisions by eliminating some options and highlighting others. It is the complementarity of feeling and thought that provides the balance to harmonise head and heart.

Learning, because it involves something new and unknown, inevitably triggers a range of emotions. New learning often includes a risk of failure and the possibility of discomfort and disorientation, as the learner struggles to make sense of new ideas. As Goleman describes it, the body experiences an emotional hijacking, where surges in the limbic system capture the rest of the brain. This can result in a feeling of helplessness and a 'down-shifting' to self-protective behaviours. It can also trigger 'flow', that feeling almost of rapture as one engages in the optimum learning experience (Csikszentmihalyi, 1990). Flow is a state where the individual is totally and unselfconsciously absorbed and engaged in the pleasure of the learning and the doing. Needless to say, people learn more and sustain their interest in the learning more when they have experienced and are motivated by experiences of 'flow' in their learning than when their learning is forced and the emotional response is fear and anxiety. This state of engagement is based on relaxed

> . . . *emotional safety is necessary for intellectual risk taking.*
> *Gipps et al. (2000)*

alertness, a combination of perceived safety and challenging learning experiences.

Learning is social

Learners are never 'tabula rasa'. They are not containers to be filled; rather, their minds are whirling, spiralling, dancing – connecting and challenging everything that they encounter. This process begins in tiny infants and, as they grow, they create coherent and (for them) reasonable patterns of the world around them. These beliefs about what the world is like come very early from interaction with the family and the community. Early experiential knowledge forms the fabric of children's lives and is often very resistant to change. It is the *stuff* that life has taught them. In the conception of learning that we described above, learners test the veracity of their beliefs and their ideas (and those of their community and culture) by comparing them to the beliefs and ideas held by the people and the culture around them. This testing process often involves books, media, teachers, parents and experts. Social interactions, formal and informal, are important contributors to learning and to the beliefs that people hold.

Vygotsky (1978) enhanced our understanding of learning as a social process. He argued that the capacity to learn from others is fundamental to human intelligence. With help from someone more knowledgeable or skilled, the learner is able to achieve more than she/he could achieve alone. Co-operation therefore lies at the heart of success.

Learning is influenced by context

Learning doesn't take place in a vacuum. It is located in a context, whether the classroom, playground, staff room, school, home, local community centre, countryside or wherever. Learning in schools, in particular, takes place in a social context that affects the learning within it (Putnam and Borko, 2000). The very nature of classroom and school settings can be more or less learning friendly. One Australian study found that classrooms that are personalised, encourage active participation and the use of investigative skills produce more meaning-oriented approaches to learning in their students (Dart *et al.*, 1999). People may also learn in one context but fail to transfer their learning to different contexts. When a subject is taught in many different contexts, however, and includes examples demonstrating broad applicability of what is taught, there is more likelihood of people being able to abstract what is relevant and construct their own knowledge to apply flexibly as the situation arises (Gick and Holyoak, 1983).

Perhaps most importantly, the learning context can influence learners' motivation and identities. Take, for example, the classroom as a learning context. Teachers' values and beliefs influence the type of structure they create in the classroom and their responses to pupils (Ames, 1992). Children are astute observers of teachers and can identify differential treatment by them (Weinstein, 1998), frequently lowering the motivation of pupils who see themselves as less able. Through detailed case studies of individual children throughout their primary schooling, Pollard and Filer (1999) demonstrate how they are continuously shaping, maintaining and actively evolving their pupil identities as they move from one classroom context to the next. What this means is that each child's or young person's sense of self as a pupil can be enhanced or threatened by changes over time in their relationships, structural position in the classroom and relative success or failure. It can also be affected by their teachers' expectations, learning and teaching strategies, classroom organisation and criteria for evaluation. As Galloway and colleagues (1998) note: 'One of the more consistent conclusions from research on school and teacher effectiveness is the overwhelming influence of the learning environment created by each teacher within her or his classroom.'

> How do learners in your school/workplace learn about their own ability in the context of different learning environments?
> When, where and how is learning taking place?
> How supportive is the learning context of your school/a school you know?

Learning is different for everyone

Each individual is unique. As with all other human characteristics, learning is diverse and different for each learner. It is a function of heredity, experiences, perspectives, backgrounds, talents, interests, capacities, needs and the unpredictable flow of any particular life. Learners have different emotional states, rates and styles of learning, stages of development, abilities, talents, feelings of efficacy, and other needs. It is exactly this diversity that provides innumerable opportunities for expanding learning – first, by acknowledging differences in physiological, personal, linguistic, cultural and social backgrounds and second, by focusing on the common features that make all of us human. But all of the differences must be taken into account to provide all learners with the necessary challenges and opportunities for learning and self-development.

For example, Howard Gardner has identified eight intelligences, only one of which is logical-rational.

Linguistic	Logical-mathematical
Musical	Bodily-kinaesthetic
Interpersonal	Spatial
Intrapersonal	Naturalist

Gardner (1999a)

What is important about Gardner's work is that it highlights that there's more than one way to be intelligent: or, as someone once said, it changes the question from 'How smart are you?' to 'How are you smart?' It also opens a window of understanding of how different people learn and how to help them learn. It doesn't mean that it's all right if someone has difficulty learning to read (linguistic) but is very musical; rather, it means that drawing on their musical intelligence may be a way to help them learn to read.

. . . And it's about time

The dramatic changes that we described in the previous chapter continue to force people to confront radical differences between what is emerging and personal beliefs or knowledge. Unlike changes in previous generations, however, those in the twenty-first century will continue at an ever-accelerating pace that necessitates more sophisticated learning, if for no other reason than to ensure human survival and adaptation.

For many years, attendance at school has been required (for children and for teachers) while learning at school has been optional. In fact, in many cultures (including England, Canada and the United States), learning has not always been a high-status activity. Schools have been largely sorting institutions to feed a hungry marketplace. It is time to bring learning into consciousness and focus our attention on making it the central issue in schools – for pupils, for teachers, for leaders and for schools as organisations. As we saw in Chapter 1, the next stage in human history is likely to require much more attention to intentional and complex learning. The mind has enormous untapped potential that we all need to learn how to use. And we already know enough about how the mind works and how learning occurs to move the human learning quotient much higher up the scale. At the same time, learning is hard work – especially learning for understanding that requires retention, organising principles and the active use of knowledge.

Learning takes time

Deep learning requires more than a good memory. It takes conscious effort and focused attention. And this takes time. As will be more evident throughout the book, all of the groups of interest will need to work hard to challenge existing beliefs, make the connections, internalise and practise new ideas and skills, and deal with the emotions that will accompany the changes. Time has become a precious resource. Educators everywhere are grappling with decisions about how to schedule it, how to use it, how to preserve it, and so on. As Clay Lafleur (2001) cautions, 'We must make choices and become increasingly ingenuous and ingenious in how we allocate scarce time'.

Negotiating uses of time is not an easy task in a world that is routinely speeding up and demanding more of everyone, always more quickly. One of the challenges of the twenty-first century will be finding ways to capture and dedicate the time necessary for the serious business of learning.

What's in it for schools?

Learning, in the final analysis, is change. It is a sophisticated process that requires high-level thinking, conceptual understanding and thoughtful decision-making, liberally peppered with reserving judgement, self-monitoring and the humility and courage to accept the discomfort of uncertainty, reflect and rethink, and continue the pursuit of clarity in understanding. It is the work of children and youths as they prepare for an exciting and fast-paced future. It is the job of teachers who are propelling themselves and guiding their pupils to create a world worth inhabiting. It is the responsibility of school leaders to move beyond the known and stretch their vision and their capacities. And finally, they all need to work together, collectively, to ensure that schools are also organisations that learn. Pupils, teachers and headteachers need to develop the knowledge and the skills to solve complex, multi-step tasks, to extract ideas from complex material, make judgements about the truth of arguments and anticipate the implications of their decisions. This kind of learning is a far cry from simple recitation and memorisation of facts and figures. It requires 'deep thought' – the kind of thought that emerges from having the freedom to pursue knowledge and possession of the intellectual tools (concepts and ideas) that allow the thinking to take place (Prawat, 1991).

> In a context where the knowledge base doubles every 300 days and the ability to learn in a wider landscape of learning is increasingly important, the focus on learning about learning stands in its own right as a key goal for schooling.
>
> Watkins (2001)

John Ralston Saul (1995) has suggested that we have become an 'unconscious civilisation' – so acculturated to the rhetoric of experts and special interest groups that we are unable to act, even when we have knowledge about the best interests of the society. He suggests that the citizenry has been marginalised by its own conformity when important decisions are being made and that democracy itself is at risk. He also identifies state education as the locus of learning in which all citizens have the opportunity to develop the skills, acquire the ideas and concepts, and practice the behaviours that will allow them access to important public debates.

> Never before has the success, perhaps even the survival of nations and people, been so tightly tied to their ability to learn.
>
> Darling-Hammond (1997)

In the next few chapters we apply these ideas, looking at the learning of pupils, teachers and leaders: what *learnings* are important, what we know about children's, adolescents' and adults' learning, how to enhance their learning, the implications for time and, fundamentally, what's in it for schools.

Further reading and network sources

Howard Gardner's *Intelligence Reframed: Multiple Intelligences for the 21st Century* is an update on his now 'eight-and-a-half' intelligences, containing useful chapters on myths and realities, and questions and answers about multiple intelligences. It is a readable volume that makes his theory more useful in schools.

The bestseller that started the international interest in emotional intelligence is Daniel Goleman's *Emotional Intelligence: Why it Can Matter More than IQ.* Goleman has also written follow-ups, including, *Working with Emotional Intelligence.*

The National School Improvement Network at London's Institute of Education (www.ioe.ac.uk/iseic) has produced a number of accessible research summaries. In *Brain Research and Learning – An Introduction*, Frank McNeil provides a relatively recent, comprehensive synthesis, raising important questions to follow up. Susan Greenfield's writing is also very reader-friendly and current, and Pat Wolfe, a staff developer, has spent years trying to understand brain research. We found her latest book – *Brain Matters: Translating Research into Classroom Practice* – a helpful addition.

David Perkins is a master at taking complex matters of learning and understanding and presenting them in ways that are useful for teachers in their daily work. In *Smart Schools* he offers very practical ideas about how to move to 'teaching for understanding'.

Living Well is an accessible introduction to Mihaly Csikszentmihalyi's 'flow' theory. In it he argues that everyday life can be an 'optimal experience'.

The Campaign for Learning offers a range of publications related to learning at work, family learning and learning to learn. Contact www.campaign-for-learning.org.uk

3 Pupil learning at the centre

This book addresses learning at many levels. In this chapter we explore learning as it relates to pupils, particularly in schools. We begin with a look at what pupils need to learn, move to current theories about learning of young children and adolescents, examine the context and conditions that support pupils' learning, and end with ways of enhancing pupil learning.

What do pupils need to learn?

The important elements of what governments believe pupils need to learn are generally defined in the curriculum of the day. At the turn of the last century, universal education emerged out of the industrial revolution as a necessity for the smooth running of the society and reflected the utilitarian purposes of the culture. The curriculum was clear but narrow. Most children needed to be able to read, write and work with numbers. Content knowledge was the *stuff* of curriculum and only some of the children needed more than these basic skills and relatively small amounts of *stuff*. The few who would hold knowledge-based positions needed considerably more of the *stuff*. Schools, therefore, not only taught basic skills to most children; they decided on the select few who would receive the stuff necessary to advance in society.

Since then, the world has become more complicated and inter-connected. Curriculum, as Valerie Bayliss (1999) suggests in *Opening Minds*, a report for the Royal Society for the Encouragement of Arts, Manufactures and Commerce (RSA), is no longer a description of the content. It is much broader and provides the learning framework for preparing young people for their adult lives. In this context, curriculum governs what happens in schools and must provide all pupils with the opportunity to develop more than the foundation skills of literacy and numeracy. It must also include advanced educational goals and sophisticated skills like thinking, solving problems, making informed judgements, distinguishing between right and wrong, working independently and in groups and handling ambiguity. The requirements for pupils who will live their lives in the twenty-first century must go far beyond the basics in both scope and sophistication.

As we noted in Chapter 1, the UNESCO report, *Learning: The Treasure Within*, argues that traditional educational responses are no longer appropriate, and that individuals need to be able to seize learning opportunities throughout life, to adapt to a changing, complex and interdependent world (Delors *et al.*, 1996). For this reason, UNESCO's International Commission identified *learning to know, learning to do, learning to live together* and *learning to be* as the pillars of learning for the future.

As the report identified, *learning to know* is only one facet of a complete human being. Schools also need to foster *learning to do, to live together* and *to be*. Moving beyond a traditional cognitive rational curriculum continues to be a major area of focus and debate in education. One such example of this is Daniel Goleman's (1996) vivid account of the need for and importance of developing skills of personal emotional awareness and an awareness of the emotions of others. But awareness is not enough. Goleman describes ways to establish competence and confidence in facing emotional turmoil and conflicts. Conflict resolution, assertiveness, active listening are but a few of the strategies that young people will require as adults.

Our own *preferred future* envisages a world in which young people possess not only competence and confidence in a broad range of areas, but also the tools to adapt to new knowledge as it comes along – 'learning power' or 'learnacy' as Patricia Broadfoot, Guy Claxton and colleagues (2001) call it – and the dispositions to function wisely and with civility in a fast-paced and unpredictable world.

Five competences for the twenty-first century

Learning – understanding how to learn; learning how to think; understanding own creative talents and using them; learning to enjoy and love learning; literacy, numeracy and spatial understanding; handling ICT and understanding underlying processes.

Citizenship – understanding: ethics and values; society, government and business, and importance of active citizenship; cultural and community diversity; social implications of technology; managing these aspects of life, including own financial affairs.

Relating to people – understanding: how to relate to people in varying contexts; how to operate in teams; how to develop other people. Developing ways of: communicating; managing personal and emotional relationships; managing stress and conflict.

Managing situations – understanding and developing ways: managing own time; managing change; celebrating success and managing disappointment; being entrepreneurial and initiative taking; managing risk and uncertainty.

Managing information – developing range of techniques for accessing, evaluating, differentiating, analysing, synthesising and applying information. Understanding importance of reflecting and applying critical judgement, and learning how to do so.

Based on Bayliss for the RSA (1999)

Understanding pupils' learning

Although the process of learning is similar at all ages, there are some fundamental differences in how learning occurs for children and youth. Some of these differences are biological and developmental; some are cognitive; others are psychological, social and emotional.

Learning in young children

Recent research suggests that infants are not 'blank slates' (Donovan *et al.*, 1999). In fact, from early infancy, children are active learners who bring a point of view to their learning. Even without language, they develop early representations of objects, space, time, causality and self. By looking, listening and touching, they gradually establish beliefs about the world around them.

Young children have early predispositions to learn about some things more than others. They give precedence to certain kinds of information (language, concepts of number, physical properties, biological concepts, and movement of animate and inanimate objects) and they construct new knowledge and understanding based on what they know on a moment-by-moment basis. Like all other learners, they draw on will, ingenuity, effort and experiences to enhance their learning. On a recent visit to the zoo the five-year-old grandson of one of us stopped at each cage to count the animals, announcing gleefully, 'There are 1, 2, 3, 4 monkeys. There are 1, 2, 3 elephants'. But he was stumped at a cage that contained 2 polar bears and 3 wolves. 'I know that there are 1, 2, 3, 4, 5 but I don't know what of. What do you call bears and wolves together?'

Two of the most fundamental building blocks of learning for pupils are literacy and numeracy. Without them, it is very difficult to learn in other areas. Virtually all other domains of learning use language and mathematics as the basis for communicating ideas, concepts, theories and models. Children need to develop concepts of language and number so that they can move from *learning how* to read, write and work with numbers to *using* reading, writing and mathematics as tools to learn in other areas. This belief forms the basis for the National Literacy and Numeracy Strategies in England. All children must become proficient in literacy and numeracy, as an entitlement. This is not to suggest that literacy and numeracy are the only building blocks for learning. They are essential for future learning but they are not all that young children need to learn, nor should they displace other important learning. Instead, they are necessary but not sufficient precursors for more complex learning. Having control over the basic communication codes of the society equips pupils to enter the rich and varied worlds of all of the traditional disciplines and any other field of knowledge that they choose to pursue. They can use the symbol systems of language and number to develop competence and expertise in other areas by engaging in the learning work of developing and internalising knowledge, organising knowledge in a broad range of areas of study and connecting ideas together in ways that make sense. This requires facility with the conventions, knowledge, concepts and ideas embedded in the particular discipline, as well as comfort with a whole range of ways of thinking about and analysing them.

Luckily, children are inherently motivated to learn. They have deep and genuine curiosity about the world around them and a determination to make sense of their environment and how it all fits together (Armstrong, 1998). As any parent or teacher knows, children are continually asking questions and putting forward hypotheses as they try to make connections that will help them understand the world around them.

> The kind of school that I envision is one that offers a special place for philosophers, for people who ask "why" questions. Nothing is more important to building a culture of inquiry and a community of learners . . . In schools, there *are* philosophers, usually the five- and six-year olds. But very soon they turn from philosophers into producers.
>
> Barth (1990)

At the same time, learning is emotional for young children. They are excited and energised by new learning and proud to share what they know and can do with others. They worry about what things mean and build conceptions about themselves and their capability in relation to the feedback that they receive about their competence and their views. Self-esteem in children is intimately tied to the extent to which the world around them makes sense, feels predictable and provides the safety and encouragement to explore and learn. How children feel about themselves also has a direct bearing on how they learn. Perhaps the most important concept they learn in their early years is about themselves: self-concept. They learn this through positive and negative interactions with significant people around them – parents or carers, siblings, neighbours, extended families and teachers. From these interactions, children build a notion of whether they are loved, capable, funny, bad, 'stupid' and so on. Learning is about taking a risk. Children who feel supported will take a risk, try, and persevere. Conversely, children who have learned they are incapable or worse will give up and may adopt deviant behaviours.

A primary school participating in the Improving School Effectiveness Project in Scotland, in which one of us was involved, was successful in significantly boosting its pupils' self-reported self-esteem over the project period (Stoll *et al.*, 2001). The school is in the east end of a large city in an extremely disadvantaged area, renowned for drug and alcohol problems. Many children come from broken homes, with many young mothers, fourth-generation unemployment, and 80 per cent of the pupils eligible for free school meals. The pupils bring violence into school with them. In justifying the school's emphasis on self-esteem, a teacher argued: 'There is no magic wand we can wave to make these children's lives better which in turn would affect their learning. Firstly we have to boost their self-esteem.' We see self-esteem and learning as intimately connected and feeding one another. Positive self-esteem encourages learning; learning enhances self-esteem.

Adolescent learning

Although adults often wonder what planet adolescents come from, their thinking is not really as bizarre as it sometimes appears. Young adolescents are facing their first identity crisis (Hargreaves *et al.*, 1996). Needless to say, they are full of both excitement and fear. Those of us who have been around a while know that there will be more, but that never makes it any less traumatic or any less exciting. So, adolescents are embroiled in establishing themselves and coming to grips with some basic structures of thinking and of their own culture. They explore the conflict between good and evil, the contrast between light and dark, the differences between fact and fiction. They use their imagination to play out all of the moral and social dilemmas that plague them in a non-threatening way. In a myriad of ways, they evaluate the social implications of their personalities (all facets of them) and explore a range of standards and values as they strive to 'become' themselves. In all of this, they are consummate 'learners', acquiring the skills, knowledge and dispositions that will form the basis for their adult lives.

Learning at this stage, like everything else about adolescents, is dramatic and 'over the top'. Nothing is static or predictable and there is tremendous variability within any group of adolescents (not to mention any particular adolescent on a given day). It is a time of paradoxes in which enormous changes are taking place and the learning curve is extremely steep. Adolescents are sitting on the cusp of adulthood, developing the intellectual skills and habits that will serve them for a lifetime, at a time when they are experiencing the greatest emotional and physical changes since infancy. They have notoriously short attention spans for many activities but are capable of concentrating on topics that interest them for long periods of time. They need lots of sleep and become walking zombies, only emerging from their stupor as night falls. They are moving from using concrete-operational thinking that deals with the here-and-now to more abstract, hypothetical, future-oriented ideas. As might be expected, they vacillate unpredictably between the two, and most of them are not yet experts at anything. They possess the reasoning ability and curiosity to learn but they lack the knowledge and experiences to see patterns and transfer ideas. They already know a great deal and they are poised to learn even more. But being a novice and building the tools for learning is particularly hard work. At the same time, they are curious about and often plagued by some of humankind's biggest questions – about life, death, love, self and truth.

As children enter adolescence, the social fabric of their learning expands as their contacts broaden and they become more closely identified with peers. Within their peer group, young adolescents encounter many new ideas and points of view. These expanded points of view often contribute to dissonance as they try to integrate and connect new ideas with old ones. Ideas and habits they may have accepted as universal, from wearing a coat to go out, to eating meat, to living in extended families, to believing in capital punishment, are laid open to challenge as they encounter different beliefs and routines. At this time in history, issues of socialisation and social identity are more complex than ever before. The forces we described in Chapter 1 are operating daily on the lives of children, so that the range of possible influences extends well beyond the people with whom they have personal contact. They have access to the world through television, internet, magazines and musical groups. Globalisation will draw them beyond their local boundaries, but tribalism may be their refuge from the unknown. Each person will be affected in unique ways. The actual influences on the society remain to be seen.

Think back to when you were adolescents. What mattered to you? What didn't matter? What irritated you? What are the implications of your responses for your work?

Creating a supportive context for pupil learning

As we have argued, learning takes place within a social context. This learning context has a significant impact in the quality and amount of learning possible. Some pupils are readier to learn than others, but schools have a particular responsibility to provide and create conditions that are instrumental in fostering learning for all children and young people. Some of these conditions are social and some are material; some happen in individual classrooms, some in playgrounds, assemblies and elsewhere around school; and others are dependent on partnerships and collaboration between those within schools and those outside.

Ethos is often used to describe the outward expression of a school's norms and values; it's a reflection of the school's deeper underlying culture (Robertson and Toal, 2001). The ethos in a school can be very conducive to learning for pupils; conversely, it can stand in the way of learning. In the early 1990s the Scottish Office published a set of ethos indicators for schools to use as a self-assessment tool.

Pupil morale	Equality and justice
Teacher morale	Extra-curricular activities
Teachers' job satisfaction	School leadership
Physical environment	Discipline
Learning context	Information to parents
Teacher–pupil relationships	Parent–teacher consultation

SOED (1992)

Elsewhere we talk about teacher morale, satisfaction, school leadership and relationships with parents and the community. Here, we highlight other key aspects of ethos.

Ensure a safe physical environment

Physical safety is a basic requirement of effective schools (Edmonds, 1979). If children, and indeed adults, do not feel safe, learning is highly unlikely. Safety is more of an issue in some areas than in others, but it demands attention in all schools. In a recent series of newspaper articles, young people were asked what schools should be like. They were clear about their first priority. Schools should be safe places to learn where no children are picked on or bullied, no one has weapons and no one gets hurt in the playground.

Nurture positive relationships

Positive relationships with teachers aren't just the icing on the cake: they are really important to pupils. Pupils care whether teachers are kind and they like teachers to know how to have fun. As some Year 5 to Year 8 pupils involved in the Learning in the Middle Years (LIMY) project in 13 Gloucestershire, Wiltshire and Swindon schools (Muschamp *et al.*, 2001) commented, when asked what makes a good teacher:

> One that's helpful, kind, generous, understanding, does not shout and can have a good laugh.

> A fun, bright, nice, helpful, funny and encouraging teacher is a good one.

> A good teacher is someone who cares for the pupils' needs and who understands if people have problems.

In short, it is important to young people that their teachers think of them as people and not just learners. Significantly, it has been found that teachers' support for learning and relationships with pupils is associated with greater pupil engagement with school (Thomas *et al.*, 2000), and there is also a link between pupils demonstrating greater academic progress and teachers showing a personal interest in them (Mortimore *et al.*, 1988).

Be fair and respectful

Pupils have a strong sense of justice. They need to feel that their teachers respect them and are fair (Rudduck *et al.*, 1996). McLaughlin and Talbert (1993) point out that children have many difficult and competing pressures of family, peers and community to navigate at the same time as being expected to function as pupils. Many of these pressures are considerably more 'adult' than the pressures their parents endured: many children and young people grow up very quickly in today's society. Along with this comes a need and, indeed, a demand to be treated with respect, as young people in the LIMY project showed when asked what makes a good teacher:

> Someone who treats you with the same respect as adults.

> Listens to us and our opinion of things.

Happy. Someone who doesn't shout at you when you say 'can you help me please' (lets you go to the toilet !!!).

Maintain high expectations

School effectiveness research consistently finds a relationship between high expectations and pupils' progress, development and achievement. We know teachers' expectations for their pupils can influence the children's future academic performance and self-perception (Pilling and Kellmer Pringle, 1978; Meyer, 1982). How it works is still not well understood, but teachers' behaviour can be affected by their expectations, and somehow they communicate their mental attitudes to children (Brophy and Good, 1970; Nash, 1973).

Compare these comments from teachers in two Scottish primary schools involved in the Improving School Effectiveness Project in Scotland. Both schools serve areas of serious deprivation. Teachers were asked, 'What are the most significant factors affecting children's ability to learn?' Responses in one school included:

> *Home background, deprivation, parental views on education. Often survival is more important than taking on board educational opportunities.*

> *Some children are never going to achieve very much..*

In contrast, in the other school, the response was:

> *. . . there are no limitations. You can come in this door and the world is your oyster . . . the children will be encouraged. Nothing is holding them back.*

This second school is the one that significantly boosted their children's self-esteem, and although one teacher in this school described pupils as 'vulnerable and they have to be able to cope with what they are doing', she added 'it doesn't mean that you don't push them further the next time'. Another colleague displayed the same firm beliefs: 'Everyone wants the children to achieve great things' (Stoll *et al.*, 2001). In a secondary school in the same project hardly any teachers agreed with the survey statement 'Teachers in this school believe all pupils can be successful' (MacBeath, 1998a). These findings reinforce that expectations can operate at a whole-school level, and that two schools with very similar intakes can have completely different beliefs about their pupils.

> . . . caring requires expectations of quality work from *all* children. To do less is uncaring. To decide that pupils cannot learn important things, like reading, because they are deprived, handicapped in some way or not academically bright, is to be uncaring and inhumane. Caring teachers expect *all* pupils to do well; they do what it takes to the best of their abilities to help each pupil achieve.
>
> Stoll and Fink (1996)

In her autobiography, *Once in a House on Fire*, Andrea Ashworth thanks one of her secondary teachers, someone who 'radiated a crucial sense of possibility'. This is the power of positive expectations and is critically important for all young people, especially those with challenging home circumstances like Andrea.

What would you see and hear in a school with high expectations?

Promote positive school behaviour

Schools have different disciplinary climates, as a study of Australian secondary schools found (Cohen and Thomas, 1984). Table 3.1 shows Cohen's and Thomas's four climates and Watkins' and Wagner's (2000) suggestions for different routes to improving school behaviour in each of these schools.

Watkins and Wagner argue that effective problem solving depends on effective problem definition. They offer a set of questions that individual teachers, groups of teachers or a whole staff might ask to help understand pupil behaviour.

- *WHAT behaviour is causing concern?* Specify clearly, do not merely re-label.
- *IN WHAT SITUATIONS does the behaviour occur?* In what settings/ contexts, with which others?

- *IN WHAT SITUATIONS does the behaviour NOT occur?* (This can often be the most illuminating question).
- *What happens BEFORE the behaviour?* A precipitating pattern? A build up? A trigger?
- *What FOLLOWS the behaviour causing concern?* Something which maintains the behaviour?
- *What SKILLS does the person demonstrate?* Social/communication skills? Learning/classroom skills?
- *What skills does the person apparently NOT demonstrate?* How may these be developed?
- *What view does the person have of their behaviour?* What does it mean to them?
- *What view does the person have of themselves?* And may their behaviour enhance that view?
- *What view do others have of the person?* How has this developed? Is it self-fulfilling? Can it change?
- *Who is most concerned by this behaviour?*

Table 3.1 Four disciplinary climates and possible improvement routes

Controlled	**Conflictual**
Characteristics	*Characteristics*
Low misbehaviour, severe punishment	**High misbehaviour, severe punishment**
Improvement route	*Improvement route*
Develop positive student self-control in the learning process	**Increase reward and shared purpose**
Libertarian	**Autonomous**
Characteristics	*Characteristics*
High misbehaviour, light punishment	**Low misbehaviour, light punishment**
Improvement route	*Improvement route*
Develop greater direction and concern for others	**Maintain concern for pupil development and active involvement in learning process**

Source: Based on Cohen and Thomas (1984), and Watkins and Wagner (2000)

Notably, schools and classrooms that have worked to develop them-selves as caring and supportive communities have been found to be important in improving behaviour (Battistich *et al.*, 1995).

> Students need to feel safe in order to take intellectual risks; they must be comfortable before they can venture into the realm of discomfort. Few things stifle creativity like the fear of being judged or humil-iated. Thus, a supportive environment will allow people of any age to play with possibilities and challenge themselves to stretch their thinking. The moral is: if you want academic excellence, you have to attend to how children feel about school and each other.
>
> Kohn (1996)

Enhancing pupil learning

In his book *Smart Schools: From Training Memory to Educating Minds*, David Perkins (1992) makes the bold statement that we already know enough about how learning works, how teachers teach and how to cope with diversity to make a much better job of education. His claim comes in response to one of the most dramatic discoveries in learning research – that being able to recall and even to apply concepts doesn't necessarily mean that the ideas have been understood. Most pupils, including the best pupils in the best schools, don't really understand (Gardner, 1991). All too often, children learn how to plug numbers into a formula or memorise descriptions of complex phenomena, but when they encounter the concepts in a new situation, they do not know how to use them. Material is kept in memory and drawn out (often erroneously) when it might fit. Unfortunately, pupils often know far more than they understand about subjects they have studied and suffer from many misconceptions or misunderstandings (Perkins and Unger, 2000).

Learning for understanding suggests a much deeper grasp of underlying ideas and concepts, not just recitation of algorithms or rules. Understanding is knowledge in action. Pupils who understand can take knowledge, concepts, skills and facts and apply them in new situations where they are appropriate. The goal, according to Perkins, is to ensure that pupils not only retain knowledge but also understand it and are able to apply it.

If the adults of tomorrow are going to have deep understanding, the teaching of today must contain many more pieces, intricately connected to one another. In particular, teaching for understanding recognises many kinds of knowledge, intelligences and learning styles. It also depends on knowledge about pupils' prior knowledge; focuses on higher-order learning and thinking; gives attention to the social and emotional nature of learning; ties learning to real life and provides a genuine role for pupils in their own learning. Here, we focus on 11 ways in which teachers and others can enhance pupils' learning.

Start with what they believe to be true

Pupils come to classrooms with preconceptions about the way the world works. If their initial understanding is not engaged, they may fail to grasp new concepts and information or may memorise material for the immediate purposes (e.g., the test) but revert to their preconceptions outside the classroom. Very often these preconceptions include stereotypes and simplifications. Nevertheless, they have a profound effect on the integration of new concepts and information. Unless teachers really figure out what pupils believe is true and confront their notions about the world, they will continue to hold on to many misconceptions, some of which will make it impossible for them ever to truly understand more complex phenomena that build on this prior knowledge.

Teaching is the vehicle for bringing the collective wisdom of the culture, as it is captured in text, video, story, etc., to bear on the issues at hand as a way of explicating and challenging existing beliefs. Teaching can take many forms from lectures to field trips, choral responses to computer simulations. The important issue is getting an accurate grasp on what pupils (individually and collectively) believe to be true and using this knowledge as a starting point for teaching, all the while monitoring pupils' changing conceptions and altering teaching to fit. Errors are the window into pupils' learning. An understanding of their incomplete understandings, false beliefs, misconceptions and naïve interpretations of concepts gives the clues for creating conditions for learning. These preconceptions must be addressed before any new learning can take place, particularly if they are inconsistent with the new knowledge and the learner must accommodate to the new information by changing beliefs. Unless the teacher can figure out what pupils believe and what would convince them that their ideas are flawed or simplistic, pupils will continue to hold onto their preconceptions.

Make connections

In an information-based society, there is an endless amount of accessible information. Pupils are faced with the enormous task of making meaning out of a sea of seemingly unrelated ideas and facts. They need mechanisms for categorising and organising information, connecting ideas and identifying or constructing patterns.

> *Learning is seeing patterns in the world around us. Teaching is creating the conditions in which pupils can see the known patterns of our collective understanding. Nobel prize winners see patterns where they have not been seen before.*
>
> John Polanyi, Nobel Laureate
> – Chemistry (1999, speaking to high-school students)

Patterning of information allows the learner to associate ideas with their prior learning and screen new information against previously developed mental hooks. Remember the story of the cats and dogs in the previous chapter. The niece in the story needed to 'see' for herself that dogs could be girls. These kinds of examples, simulations, experiments, explorations, etc. are vehicles for helping children confront their own faulty beliefs and begin to construct new (and hopefully more accurate) ones.

Helping children to connect different aspects of their knowledge together and with new information is an extremely important role for teachers. They can also help children build on their existing knowledge and competencies by providing supporting structures or 'scaffolds' for learning. These scaffolding activities keep the pupils focused and show them where they are going, while keeping the immediate task manageable and attainable.

Scaffolding
- Interest the child in the task
- Reduce the number of steps required by simplifying the task into its component parts
- Maintain the pursuit of the goal and the direction of the activity toward the goal
- Mark critical features of discrepancies

- Control frustration and risk
- Demonstrate an idealised version of the outcome.

Brandsford *et al.* (1999)

Studies of effective teachers of numeracy (Askew *et al.*, 1997) and literacy (Medwell *et al.*, 1998) in young children found that the most effective teachers had a 'connectionist' orientation to teaching. They encouraged children to think and talk about what they were doing and make connections between different areas and aspects of the subjects.

Keep them engaged and motivated

Motivation has always been a central factor in learning. Very simply, motivation affects the amount of time and energy pupils are willing to devote to any task. Much of what we currently know about motivation to learn, however, is contrary to the folk wisdom of the past. For example, learning is not primarily dependent on rewards. Motivation can come from extrinsic rewards or punishments or from intrinsic interest and a 'need to know'. Humans consistently seek new experiences and follow their curiosity without extrinsic rewards. In education, marks are often used as the ultimate motivator but they have been found to be motivating for some pupils and demotivating for others (Stiggins, 1997). Motivation varies across disciplines, circumstances and time. It isn't a singular entity but is tied to interest and engagement. Pupils can be motivated by some activities or learning and not by others. Motivation is a personal phenomenon. Pupils can be momentarily apathetic or mired in chronic 'learned helplessness' (Seligman, 1975). All of these subtleties of motivation suggest that motivating learners is a complex and idiosyncratic activity with many possible solutions. Young people need to know why they are learning something and what difference it can make for them. Their motivation to learn is related to the amount of connection to their own experience or to experiences they can imagine and also to the amount of risk that the learning poses for them. They are particularly motivated by exploring and engaging in activities with an impact on others or rooted in social issues. Young people are fascinated by projects that take them into the community, allow them to work in groups, influence real decisions and challenge them to develop skills and knowledge that other people clearly value (Hargreaves *et al.*, 1996).

When pupils are in 'flow', as Csikszentmihalyi (1990) describes it, they are completely absorbed in the task at hand and will work hard and unflaggingly towards a goal, no matter how hard the new learning might be. On the other hand, if the work is boring and undemanding or if the risk of failure and embarrassment is too high, young people quickly fill the time with activities they find more compelling, often to the chagrin of the adults around them.

If motivation is essential for the hard work of learning, pupils need reasons to expend the energy. Even when they find the content interesting and activity enjoyable, learning requires sustained concentration and effort. The cognitive demand of any new learning is a cost that has to be offset.

We suggest that motivation can be stimulated and sustained through a combination of socialisation, relevance, challenge and imagination.

Socialisation

Because school attendance is compulsory and the curriculum isn't based on their particular interests or wants, pupils aren't always motivated. Some may be bored, others frustrated. In addition, pupils enter school already well socialised by the long-standing history of schools as places where they are judged and marked, often with important consequences (from parental reactions to entry to further and higher education). These factors tend to focus pupil attention on meeting demands rather than on any intangible personal benefits of the learning. Motivation to learn is something teachers can foster. They can unleash pupils' natural curiosity and encourage them to engage in classroom activities with eagerness and the intention of acquiring knowledge or skills. This involves developing the dispositions and habits of mind of taking learning seriously, recognising the value of learning and trying to get benefits from learning activities. These kinds of dispositions don't appear overnight. Like all socialising activities, they develop gradually through exposure to learning opportunities and socialising influences. Teachers can encourage and stimulate motivation to learn by providing models of valuing learning, fostering self-awareness and helping pupils understand their learning (meta-learning), teaching them strategies for successful learning, making connections among learning activities and future goals, and demonstrating and modelling reflection on learning.

Over the long run, these activities should have the cumulative effect of encouraging pupils to develop motivation to learn as an enduring disposition.

Relevance

It's hard to imagine that a 100-year-old conception of curriculum, created for another time, continues to be relevant for pupils who will live most of their lives in the twenty-first century. Many groups are revisiting the curriculum and asking challenging questions about the purpose of schooling and the best organisers for pupil learning. Debates are raging and there is no agreement about what constitutes the 'best' curriculum. We believe that relevance is one of the critical elements in discussions about curriculum. When the curriculum capitalises on students' interests, enthusiasm and talents and provides images of the world that lies ahead of them, it is much more likely to engage and inspire them so that the learning is itself the motivator.

Similarly, if connections are made between the curriculum and pupils' daily lives – whether by looking at today's parallels for King Lear's behaviour or comparing Mozart's life with that of a current popular composer – pupils are more likely to see the relevance for them.

Challenge

A relevant curriculum or a curriculum that requires imagination isn't a less ambitious or an easy curriculum. In fact, there is no excuse for watering down or deskilling the curriculum. Pupils are likely to need more skills, to be better thinkers, to be more flexible and to tolerate ambiguity and uncertainty most of the time. They need to be confident that they can handle whatever they encounter. Pupils learn best when they are in a context that provides moderate challenge. When the task is too difficult, pupils may feel threatened and 'downshift' into self-protection mode. When the task is too simple, pupils may coast into inattention and boredom (Jensen, 1998). A task is appropriately challenging when pupils are expected to risk and move into the unknown but they know how to get started and have support for reaching the new level of learning. This is what Vygotsky (1978) called the 'zone of proximal development' – that zone of competence that learners can navigate with support and that they are able to negotiate successfully with reasonable effort. A challenging curriculum engages pupils in developing skills and processes that are substantial, important and make them feel competent. It isn't so obscure, difficult or complicated that most pupils lose interest or find it impenetrable. Challenge can come with new materials, adding a degree of difficulty or changing the available resources. A challenging curriculum fosters a feeling of facing and successfully incorporating some genuine learning and experiencing 'flow' – the kind of engagement in any learning or task that is so focused and so absorbing that everything else disappears: the kind of learning that really feels good.

Imagination

Imagination and fantasy offer ready-made access to the minds of pupils and a vehicle for making learning more attractive than books or lectures. Children have vivid imaginations that allow them to see many possibilities in their minds that aren't available to them in real life. A curriculum based on imagination can arouse this natural interest and passion in children. It can capitalise on children's sense of wonder, extend their creativity and give them practice in making novel connections between disparate things or seeing things in ways that might be missed by the typical way of viewing life (Armstrong, 1998).

It is particularly interesting that, as less and less of what we know or have come to accept as known remains stable and unchallenged, imagination may well be a critical faculty for pupils to develop, as they confront the world as it really is – a whole series of messy, seemingly insoluble problems to unravel, explore and try to solve.

Enhancing student motivation

- Use co-operative learning rather than competitive learning.
- Stimulate cognitive conflict.
- Encourage moderate risk-taking.
- Praise good work.
- Make academic tasks interesting.
- Provide feedback that is connected to learning and effort.
- Identify many intelligences and showing that they are not fixed but incremental.
- Encourage self-images as learners.

- Increase student self-efficacy.
- Encourage volition.

Adapted from Brophy (1998)

Foster independent learning

There is often a strong sense that young people (especially adolescents) need to be contained and managed or they will erupt and spin totally out of control. Just at the time when it is essential for them to experiment with independence in safe conditions, adolescents experience tighter rules and intensified control. Independence isn't something that just occurs. Like all other complex human skills, becoming independent requires the availability of good models, explicit teaching and lots of practice. It doesn't happen immediately and there may be lots of setbacks along the way. When teachers work to involve pupils and to promote independence, they are really teaching them to be responsible for their own learning and giving them the tools to undertake it wisely and well. Pupils need to be able to experiment with new ideas, try them on, see how they fit, struggle with the misfits, and come to grips with them. They need to know the goals and the expectations, as a reference point for their learning work. This requires lots of time to practise, reflect, argue and try again. It also means teachers need to be explicit about the link between learning and specific initiatives, as Bullock and Wikeley (2001) found in their evaluation of an initiative with Year 9 pupils. They conclude: 'if learning is to be the major focus of action planning initiatives then such links between learning and the process and product need to be central to the preparation and planning from the outset. Strategies for learning are not likely to arise incidentally as a bi-product [*sic*] from an exercise focussed on other outcomes.'

Make learning social

Although learning may happen for each person individually, it doesn't happen in isolation. Pupils learn a great deal from one another and from others around them, and for many, learning with peers is critical, as pupils involved in the LIMY project reflected when asked what helps their learning:

I find working in groups are good because you all work together and everyone has ideas to voice.

Discussing things with a partner. Working in groups . . . not working in silence.

Friends to help me.

If teachers and textbooks are the only source of nourishment, it makes a pretty bland meal (not to mention an unbalanced diet). Knowledge is often constructed during shared experiences, through the interplay of many minds confronting a challenge together. Social engagement can provide a powerful vehicle for learning. The concept of a learning community is an important one for pupils to grasp. Co-operative cultures and group investigation methods allow pupils to process ideas and deal with beliefs, conceptions, inconsistencies and misconceptions out loud, with their peers. Learning is enhanced when pupils learn how to learn together, engage in serious discussion about and examination of important topics, have shared responsibility for applying what they know to new situations, and use the time to raise questions and to monitor their own learning, individually and as a group.

Teachers are also part of the social milieu of the classroom. They are important reference points for pupil learning, even in activities as simple as reacting appropriately to correct and incorrect answers and engaging pupils in interactions about the issues under study. Ongoing feedback and engagement with pupils create the connections, provide the social safety net that allows pupils to take risks in their learning, and give teachers opportunities to add to the discussions from their expert knowledge.

Analysing more than 120 studies that took place over almost 60 years, Johnson and his colleagues (1982) found that co-operative learning experiences tend to promote higher-level achievement than competitive and individualistic learning experiences. This held true for all ages, subject areas and tasks, including problem solving. Significantly, they found that discussion involved promoted discovery and development of higher-quality cognitive strategies, and involved participants in conflicts that required skilful management. This led to

Table 3.2 Differences between co-operative and 'traditional' learning groups

Co-operative learning groups	Traditionally learning groups
Positive interdependence – concerned with performance of whole group	No interdependence
Accountability of each individual for their contribution	Not individual accountability
Heterogeneous membership – ability and personal characteristics	Homogenous membership
Shared leadership for each other's learning	One leader
Shared responsibility	Responsibility only for self
Working relationships important (group maintenance) as well as maximising learning (task)	Only task emphasised
Social skills directly taught	Social skills assumed and ignored
Teacher observes and intervenes	Teacher ignores group functioning
Groups process their effectiveness	No group processing

Source: Johnson and colleagues (1984)

increased motivation, more regular oral rehearsal and repetition, peer feedback, regulation support, development of liking for each other and encouragement.

Johnson and colleagues (1984) provide a useful framework for looking at the differences between co-operative learning groups and what they describe as 'traditional' learning groups (see Table 3.2).

What kinds of learning groups exist in your school(s)?

Capitalise on pupils' diversity

Children come to school with their unique talents, experiences and backgrounds. They have many things in common but they also have an array of differences that make them individuals. Teachers are faced with the paradox of providing high-quality experiences to foster the learning of each child while, at the same time, adhering to the National Curriculum and having high standards for all. Teachers who recognise the inherent and inevitable diversity in every classroom organise their teaching and develop strategies for negotiating the distance between the curriculum and each child by capitalising on the diversity and differentiating teaching for particular pupils. As Tomlinson (1999) describes it, teachers in differentiated classrooms begin where the students are, not at the front of the curriculum guide. They differentiate learning through different learning modalities, appeal to different interests, vary the pace of teaching, adapt their teaching to allow each child to learn as deeply and quickly as possible, hold all pupils to high standards, and ensure that pupils realise that success is likely to follow hard work. This kind of teaching requires that teachers have a clear and solid sense of what constitutes powerful curriculum and teaching and that they have the capacity to modify their teaching so that each learner comes away with the knowledge and skills for the next phase of learning. This does not necessarily mean one-to-one curriculum planning and teaching. Even within seemingly rigid structures like the literacy hour or the daily mathematics lesson, the onus is on the teacher to select the right resources, teach using appropriate strategies, organise groups and group work to suit the particular pupils in the class, and assess pupils' learning to decide about the next steps. Diversity is not a new phenomenon in schools. Children have always been unique. The novelty is in explicitly operating in ways that address the diversity that exists.

One powerful way for teachers to adapt to the diversity of their pupils is to draw on the vast array of different materials that are available and select the best medium for the pupils in the class. A teacher in a study of curriculum reform in Ontario described his approach: 'This class is really musical. So we studied *Tale of Two Cities* in novel study. We talked about and compared the justice systems in social studies. We also went to see Les Miserables. Each group in the class did a project connected to one of the key themes. They were great. One group even wrote an operetta.'

Create a short unit for pupils on 'learning about learning', which includes teaching them the theory about multiple intelligences.

Use technology as a learning tool

The availability of technology holds the promise of enlarging the range of ways in which teachers can expand their repertoire for engaging pupils' imagination and challenge their uncontested beliefs. ICT, on its own, will not transform pupil learning. Nevertheless, it offers a powerful tool for expanding the opportunities for pupils to explore the world both imaginary and real. Using ICT as a learning tool means that learners are actively participating in and contributing to their own learning, as they find, interpret and evaluate information, drawing on problem-solving and critical-thinking skills.

Technology can help pupils to understand and find answers to questions that interest them. Indeed, technology has produced a new kind of pupil: one who is familiar with microprocessors and not afraid to venture on the information superhighway. They have access to multiple sources of information and many ways to organise and structure knowledge. When coupled with skills of investigation and critical analysis, technology is a powerful tool for pupils to explore and understand the world around them. On its own, however, technology may result in too much information and too few ideas. Technologically literate pupils should be skilful, reflective, mindful users of information, not over-stimulated dilettantes without the intellectual tools to evaluate the data available to them.

Some teachers will inevitably feel the frustration associated with children who are more ICT literate than they are. Indeed, all of the young learners close to our hearts have grown up with computers and all but the very youngest are surfing the net. Nonetheless, as Angela McFarlane (1997) points out: 'As with any learning scenario, effective teaching is pivotal to the process of learning: knowing what to ask, and when, is essential.'

Foster thinking

Learning requires that pupils use their minds to unravel ideas and see patterns. All too often they are expected to think without having learned *how* to think or having practised thinking. Thinking, however, is a multi-faceted, complex neural activity that requires a range of prior skill development. Americans Art Costa and Bena Kallick (2000) have produced a series of books focused on what they call 'habits of mind'. The basic premise is that young people (and adults, for that matter) can come to deeper understanding and do much better on critical and creative thinking tasks when they are taught and internalise these habits of mind. Simply, habits of mind are 'broad, enduring and essential lifespan learnings'. So far they have identified 16 habits of mind. These include persistence, listening with understanding and empathy, questioning and posing problems, applying past knowledge to new situations, gathering data through all of the senses, and creating, imagining and innovating. In the UK, cognitive acceleration programmes in science and maths have demonstrated benefits to pupils' learning outcomes. On the basis of their evaluations, the originators, Philip Adey and Michael Shayer (1994) argue: 'You can raise standards substantially only by improving the quality of thinking. This can be done, and we have seen how raised levels of thinking open up opportunities to all children to benefit anew from good instructional practice.'

> Developing thinking requires that children are given the time and opportunity to talk about thinking processes, to make their own thought processes more explicit thus enabling them to clarify and reflect upon their strategies and gain more self-control.
>
> McGuinness (1999)

The habits of mind obviously do not replace standard curriculum or teaching. They complement and extend it by explicitly pushing the limits on pupils' thinking and equipping them with tools to go the distance in school and in life.

Assess for learning

Assessment has always served a range of purposes, sometimes completely incompatible with one another. The most prevalent purpose, however, has been *assessment of learning* – judgements about pupils' achievement and decisions about progress and placement. If learning becomes paramount in schools, the purpose of assessment changes with it – to *assessment for learning* (Assessment Reform Group, 1999). Assessment becomes an integral part of learning that provides a window into pupils' thinking for teachers and pupils and feedback to support learning. This notion of assessment for learning is central to enhancing pupil learning.

Just accepting the need for a shift is not enough, however. Thinking isn't a tangible entity and it isn't possible to see learning. Thinking and learning are abstract concepts that symbolise very complex constellations of neurological, sociological and psychological relationships. Assessment can be the vehicle for making pupils' learning visible and for communicating about it. Carefully constructed assessment tasks provide invaluable information about what a child believes to be true (e.g., all cats are girls and dogs are boys) as a starting point for teaching, creating the conditions to support learning and providing feedback to pupils about their learning.

Feedback can be evaluative or it can be descriptive. Providing feedback can take many forms.

Feedback Strategies

Evaluative feedback
- Giving rewards and punishments
- Expressing approval and disapproval

Descriptive feedback
- Telling children they are right or wrong
- Describing why an answer is correct
- Telling children what they have achieved and have not achieved
- Specifying or implying a better way of doing something
- Getting children to suggest ways they can improve.

Gipps *et al.* (2000)

A good deal of research in England and beyond is establishing the critical role of classroom assessment and feedback in pupil learning (Black and Wiliam, 1998a). When teachers use their judgements about pupils' knowledge or understanding to feed back into the teaching and learning process, they move from making decisions about pupils to providing descriptions of pupil performance and sharing the decision-making. Assessment criteria become visible and pupils (and their parents) become potential partners in the learning process (Gipps, 1994; Earl and Cousins, 1995; Stiggins, 1997).

Perhaps the most salient and exciting product of assessment for learning happens when pupils monitor their own learning and make adjustments by deciding what worked and what needs to be revisited. Becoming skilled at meta-cognition requires focused teaching, lots of examples and a great deal of practice. Nevertheless, when pupils have developed proficiency with monitoring their own learning and identifying what they need next, they are more able to transfer their learning to new settings and events, to have deeper understanding and to build the habits of mind that make them lifelong learners.

Factors in improving learning through assessment
- Effective feedback to pupils
- Active involvement of pupils in their own learning
- Adjusting teaching to take account of assessment results
- Recognition of influence of assessment on pupil motivation and self-esteem
- Self-monitoring and correction by pupils

Black and Wiliam (1998b)

Musing on the emergence of what she describes as 'a new assessment discourse', in which the preoccupation is with learning rather than with dependable measurement, Broadfoot (1996) states, 'To measure or to learn: that is the question'.

Involve pupils in their own learning

All of what we have described in this chapter points to a basic tenet – pupils learn when they are actively engaged in and responsible for their own learning. Serious involvement of pupils in their own learning means more than just giving them a voice. It means more than them being involved in year and school councils, governing bodies, peer counselling, and student curriculum evaluation groups participating in departmental unit and course reviews. Involving pupils in their learning changes the nature of the pupil/teacher relationship, such that the commitment to teaching and learning is a genuinely shared responsibility (Fielding, 2001b). The difference between pupils being co-researchers with teachers and being researchers themselves, Fielding argues, is that in the co-researcher relationship, the teachers choose what to research. When pupils are researchers they might, for example, run a session for staff on how to engage pupils with particular learning styles, suggest new units of work, or even review a particular life-skills programme.

Extend opportunities and locations for learning

Although this book is primarily about learning in schools, young people are learning wherever they are. They learn from their families, their peers, the media and the communities in which they live. The nature and breadth of the milieu in which young people learn has a very powerful influence on them. The community is not just where children learn; it is the basic fabric of their learning and contains the values, beliefs, norms, habits and behaviours of their culture and their ancestors. From a very young age, they learn through immersion in all of the subtle and overt cues that pervade the community in which they live.

Learning opportunities for some children, however, are more limited because the wider system within which schools exist has an enhancing and constraining role on their capacity to be all things to all children. To enhance learning and raise standards, therefore, it is important to work on what happens outside school as well as inside school. We discuss this in more detail in Chapter 7. Study-support initiatives within the community, however, provide a range of possibilities for involving the community in extending learning out of school hours. There are study centres in schools, community centres, churches and mosques. One example is a major initiative that began in Glasgow in late 1999 to turn libraries into 'REAL centres', community learning resources for all ages, places for children and young people to do homework, study, learn together and learn across ages and generations. Evaluation of the 'Playing for Success' study centres in Premiership football clubs demonstrates that children can be motivated to learn out of hours (NFER, 2000). Furthermore, evaluations of study support have repeatedly shown that the informal out-of-hours context is often more appealing and a more congenial context for learning than the classroom (MacBeath *et al.*, 2001; NFER, 2000). As Milbrey McLaughlin (2001) has found, the students participating in community-based organisations accomplished more than many in society would expect and more than many of them ever thought possible.

Figure 3.1 summarises what schools need to do to create the context for pupils' learning and to enhance it. They also need to make time.

Figure 3.1 Creating the context and enhancing pupil learning

. . . And it's about time

Since universal education was established, schools have served many different purposes. They have been the venues for socialisation and acculturation of the masses, purveyors of knowledge, places for developing skills, convenient holding facilities for irascible young people until they are ready to unleash on society and gatekeepers of entry into privileged positions and futures.

Most countries require that pupils go to school for 150–200 days a year and the school day lasts six to seven hours. This translates into somewhere between 900 and 1400 hours a year in school – certainly a major portion of their lives. But how much of that time is dedicated to learning? In a study conducted in Chicago in 1998, the researchers were surprised to find that of what appears to be a substantial amount of time (900 hours) only a small portion (125 hours) was dedicated to teaching and learning. The reduction arose through combinations of special days, problem days, management tasks and inefficient use of time. In some US states children spend up to 15 days a year

> *What children need is ten per cent 'Eureka time' when they can be left alone to use their own imagination; a time when target setting consists of maps of possibilities, where record keeping can consist of speculation . . .*
> *Almond (1999, cited in Abbott and Ryan, 2000)*

involved in external testing for district, state and federal governments.

A secondary pupil involved in John MacBeath and colleagues' (2000) European study of self-evaluation in schools kept detailed notes about individual lessons, itemising time spent in class, with a judgement of how much of the time was 'good learning time'. In Table 3.3 the evidence she collected in her geography lesson is shown.

Table 3.3 'Good learning time'

Activity	Class time	Good learning time
Settling in before lesson begins	4 minutes	0 minutes
Teacher listens to excuses for no homework	4 minutes	0 minutes
Teacher explains the problem of transport networks in Thailand during Vietnam War	11 minutes	4 minutes
Reading a passage and writing answers to questions	9 minutes	6 minutes
Getting into groups, discussing what we're going to do	3 minutes	1 minute
Problem solving on building road networks and airports in Thailand for military purposes	8 minutes	7 minutes
Report back from first group and class discussion	9 minutes	5 minutes plus 3 good minutes
Bell about to go, homework given out and a few questions about it	3 minutes	2 minutes

Source: MacBeath *et al.* (2000)

In the evaluation of the National Literacy and Numeracy Strategies, in which one of us is involved, we suggest that the early gains in pupil learning may be a function of changes in teaching practice that are important but relatively easy to implement, including increasing the time spent teaching literacy and numeracy.

Teachers, school leaders and policy makers may need to evaluate the ways in which their decisions contribute to the use of time in classrooms. Pupils deserve to have access to concentrated and focused periods of uninterrupted learning time. As Dimmock (2000) argues: 'The introduction of new conceptions of learning and teaching, involving higher-order thinking skills, renders the standard lesson time obsolete and inadequate. Problem-solving activities, for example, may take considerably longer than forty minutes . . . Flexible lesson time is necessary for self-paced learning.'

- Is enough class time devoted to learning as opposed to administration, discipline, settling in/packing up?
- How many class hours are lost for any reason?
- How wide are the inequalities of learning time between most and least able pupils?
- How much time do pupils spend on homework? Is it learning time?

(Based on MacBeath *et al.*, 2000)

More radical changes to use of time have been suggested by Clive Dimmock (2000), including offering more flexibility for groupings of different sizes by: 'Introducing flexitime for teachers, restructuring the curriculum to cycles of between six and nine days, dividing the school day in two parts, so that one-teacher-per-class activities take place in one half and whole-school or sub-school activities take place in the other'.

What's in it for schools?

We are proposing that pupil learning is *the* purpose of schools or should be. It is no longer sufficient for schools to sort pupils into those who need to learn a lot, some or a little. Instead, learning must be the fundamental purpose of schooling – high-level and broad learning for all pupils.

What sounds like such a simple concept has enormous and far-reaching implications for government, LEAs, schools and classrooms. All too often, schools are driven by historical views of what they are for and how they should operate. The more we learn about learning, the more likely it is that the historical vision of schools is inadequate. If learning is an active process of putting ideas together like puzzle pieces, schools must be places that offer a multitude of conditions where pupil learning can happen. Teachers can play a critical role in creating schools for learning as a move towards their preferred futures. How? By being consummate learners themselves.

Further reading and network sources

A secondary headteacher recommended Andrea Ashworth's *Once in a House on Fire*. It's a powerful autobiography, highlighting the challenges to learning and the potentially powerful impact of teachers.

Paul Black and Dylan Wiliam at Kings College and the Assessment Reform Group have produced two short and accessible documents, *Inside the Black Box* and *Beyond the Black Box*, which bullet point the conditions for using formative assessment for success in the classroom.

Network Educational Press's *School Effectiveness Series*, edited by Tim Brighouse, offers several practical learning-focused resources for teachers. Titles include Weatherley, *Leading the Learning School*, and Bishop and Denley, *Effective Learning in Science*.

Thomas Armstrong's *Multiple Intelligences in the Classroom* contains many useful ideas on exploring your own and pupils' intelligences, and incorporating multiple intelligences into lessons.

Unlocking Formative Assessment, by Shirley Clarke, provides practical strategies for enhancing pupils' learning in the primary classroom.

The Scottish Schools Ethos Network – www.ethosnet.co.uk – is a communication service between school- and home-focused educators, where members exchange ideas and experiences about evaluating school ethos from various perspectives and subsequent planned action to improve practice in schools.

David and Roger Johnson and colleagues in the United States have been exploring co-operative learning for many years. *Circles of Learning* is a short book full of practical strategies for implementing co-operative learning, as well as the research on which this is based.

Antidote (www.antidote.org.uk) provides information on how to establish emotional literacy in schools, and has a list of linked websites.

The Learning Files are a teaching resource on learning skills, written and evaluated by a classroom teacher, for upper primary and lower to middle secondary classrooms. They come in the form of 120 overhead transparencies. There are also Science and Primary Learning Files. They can all be viewed at www.learningfilescotland.co.uk

The National Pyramid Trust (NPT) (www.nptrust.org.uk) has a programme for 7–9-year-olds, involving identifying emotional and social problems and running therapeutic activity clubs, working with local partners.

4 Teachers on a learning curve

Do you remember the story of the little train that starts going up the hill very slowly, saying with great effort, 'I th-i-nk I can . . . I th-i-nk I can'? Gradually it gathers speed – 'I think I can, I think I can, I think I can' – and as it reaches the brow of the hill and rushes down the other side, it calls out much more quickly, bursting with exhilaration, 'I knew I could, I knew I could, I knew I could'. That is, of course, until it reaches the next hill! So it is with learning: it's a challenge requiring effort. With determination we reach the top of one hill, and should feel great about it, but know in all honesty there's a curve ahead of us followed by another hill. Some people seem to view everyday events as opportunities for learning: they enjoy the challenge. For example, not so long ago, when one of us asked her father, in his late eighties, about his day, he told her that on his walk he decided to go down a particular street because 'I haven't been down it before and I want to find out about it'. Another of us, as a girl, was advised by her mother that in life if she went past doors without opening them to see what was inside, she might miss something important. Both these adults demonstrate how learning needn't stop at the end of one's official education any more than lifelong learning begins at age 16.

> *If I learn something new I actually go to bed happy.*
> John Cleese (interviewed by Michael Parkinson)

Busy, overworked teachers have a huge amount to juggle in their lives: information overload; new curricula and teaching strategies to master; increasing demands for paperwork; challenging pupils; and more people

In schools we spend a great deal of time placing oxygen masks on other people's faces while we ourselves are suffocating. . . Teachers badly want their students to learn to perform . . . yet seldom reveal themselves to children as learners.

Barth (1990)

wanting pieces of them. We have already explored the imperative for learning, considering what we know about learning and particularly the learning of children and adolescents. We now turn our lens to examine teachers and their learning. Our rationale is simple. While young people spend only a relatively small proportion of their lives in school, there is no question, as school effectiveness researchers have shown, that *School Matters* (Mortimore *et al.*, 1988). In particular, what goes on between pupils and their teachers is critical to their progress and development. Teachers are at the heart of school improvement, and with all the change in the world and new understandings about learning, it is essential that they, too, keep learning.

What do teachers need to learn?

We start looking at teachers' learning by asking the question: What are the necessary learnings for teachers to be prepared for the challenge of educating young people in the twenty-first century? We think there are seven key learnings.

Understanding learning

The message for teachers from the previous two chapters is that there is a tremendous amount of new knowledge about learning, and more still to be discovered, for example on the brain. What we do know suggests very strongly that to focus on the 'tools' of teaching without an understanding of learning is shortsighted. Learning needs to come first.

Content knowledge

Teachers, like everyone else, need to be able to keep up with the rapidly increasing knowledge base and update their own organisational mental maps. Even when there is a moratorium on changing the curriculum, we are faced every day with new knowledge, some of which renders old knowledge obsolete. In particular, teachers need a detailed and deep knowledge of their own subject discipline(s).

Pedagogical understanding

To us, pedagogical understanding is about putting understanding learning and content knowledge together to develop effective teaching. 'Expert' teachers don't only have a deep knowledge of pedagogy. They can also apply what they know about how the diversity in pupils' strengths, weaknesses, home background, cultural experiences, ages (issues of child and adolescent development) and learning styles influences their learning, and how this knowledge interacts with their own classroom context. This includes being able to use 'tricks of the trade' they have developed through a range of learning opportunities, including experimenting with their own practice, to enhance pupils' learning.

Emotional understanding

As we highlighted in Chapter 2, learning is emotional. Teachers need to learn how to read the emotional responses of those around them and create emotional engagements and bonds with and among pupils. Emotional understanding requires teachers to be responsive to pupils' varied cultures, and ready to involve their families and communities in lifting learning to higher levels. As Askew and Carnell (1998) point out: 'As we enter a new millennium, emotional literacy has become more important. In relationships the need for listening, being able to negotiate difference and resolve conflict, empathize and repair difficulties, is increasingly necessary'.

Teachers also need to be aware of their own emotional responses and how they influence teaching and learning. A pupil in a study in Ontario told one of us that school was no fun any more because:

the teachers are so grumpy. They don't care about us.

How teachers feel affects their work.

Fundamentals of change

Teachers need to know what may be coming down the pipeline – probable futures. It is important for them to understand these so they can help pupils prepare for specific changes and for a future where they will need to be flexible and adaptable. It is equally important for teachers to understand the change process, which is highly complex and can be fraught with difficulties. Understanding and managing change means learning about handling uncertainty, relationships and conflict.

> Those skilled in change are appreciative of its semi-predictable and volatile character, and they are explicitly concerned with the pursuit of ideas and competencies for coping with and influencing more and more aspects of the process towards some desired set of results. They are open, moreover, to discovering new ends as the journey unfolds.
>
> Fullan (1993)

New professionalism

In today's world, classroom learning is fundamentally influenced by what goes on in and beyond the school. Teaching and learning depends on support and input from a wide range of people. Being a teacher today includes:

- teaching and related responsibilities
- being part of a larger learning community and working with others
- having collective responsibility for all pupils and helping them make connections
- reaching out to parents and the community and engaging them in different and meaningful ways
- taking responsibility for one's own continuing professional development, supported by the school
- having an inquiry-oriented approach to one's job.

Meta-learning

If 'it's about learning', teachers need to understand their own learning and internalise learning as a 'habit of mind'. This not only means showing pupils they are also learners, but having a willingness to engage in in-depth explorations of their own learning – what motivates and influences it, what hinders it, and what it feels like to be on that learning curve. We could have included this in the first learning, but chose to separate it because of the importance we ascribe to teachers and all of us working with and for young people understanding our own learning.

Adults, in some ways, are very similar to young people in terms of their orientations to learning, but they are different from them in important ways. What, then, is known about adult learners and, more specifically, about teachers as learners?

Understanding teachers' learning

Schools are geared to think about pupils' learning. It is assumed that teachers' learning is important, but how teachers learn and what influences whether they do or don't learn is often taken for granted. For example, if the staff of a school want to introduce a new way of developing pupils' critical-thinking skills, or even if just a few teachers determine that they'd like to learn a new co-operative group-work strategy, one or two teachers usually go to a short workshop, and the school expects the course's content to spread magically through the entire staff. Then, everyone is surprised when it doesn't! An alternative way to think about helping teachers change their practice and teacher learning more generally is by asking two questions: How does adult learning differ from young people's learning? What influences teacher learning? Answering these questions is likely to lead to a successful answer to the question: In what ways can teacher learning be enhanced?

How are adult learners different from young learners?

As we understand more about the brain, the mind, the impact of emotions on learning, and the relationship between motivation and learning, we are increasingly aware of many similarities in the way that children and adults learn. Guidelines such as the American Psychological Association's (1993) 'learner-centered psychological principles', for example, are intended to apply to all learners, whether children, young people, teachers, school leaders, parents, or community members involved in the educational system. A number of adult-learning theories, however, have been offered. Sharan Merriam and Rosemary Caffarella (1999) usefully highlight ways in which learning in adulthood might be distinguished from learning in childhood, focusing on the learner, the context and the learning process (see Table 4.1).

It is clear that adults must make an active choice to engage in learning. We have been influenced by Mihaly Csikszentmihalyi's (1990) metaphor of 'flow' to describe optimal learning. A person can be seen to be in flow when their goals are clear, immediate and relevant feedback is provided, and when a person's skills are completely engaged in overcoming a particular challenge that is just about manageable.

> . . . *the flow experience acts as a magnet for learning – that is, for developing new levels of challenges and skills.*
>
> Csikszentmihalyi (1997)

One of us heard echoes of these points about learning in adulthood, when she asked a group of teachers to think of a successful professional

Table 4.1 Differences between adult and young learners

The learner	Adults have richer life experiences, for drawing on as resources, but which could become greater obstacles. The developmental processes of adults are related to different life transitions e.g. parenthood, rather than physical maturation.
The context	Adults are more independent, having assumed responsibility for managing their own lives, and they have taken on social roles. Adults' lives are bounded by family, work and community, which means that learning is an extra, while children's lives are bounded mainly by home and school, and learning is their full-time job. Adults have differential access to formal learning, especially related to background, class, finances, gender etc., while school is mandatory for children.
The learning process	Adults are not inclined to engage in learning unless it is meaningful to them, while children have been conditioned by school to learn material not immediately relevant.

Source: Based on Merriam and Caffarella (1999)

learning experience they had and to answer the questions: Why was it successful? What helped you to learn? The factors they mentioned are listed below.

convinced that learning had merit
learnt from failure
clear goals
had the opportunity to process
involved regular,
non-threatening feedback
drawing from research and
grounding my own ideas
a problem to be solved (e.g. using a
computer, dealing with a disruptive
pupil)

strong motivation
support from peers
practical/useful
there was humour involved
included self-evaluation

Try this task yourself. Why was *your* professional learning experience successful? What helped *you* to learn?

What influences teacher learners?

Teachers are influenced by what goes on inside and outside them. Influences on teachers' learning aren't discrete: they can't be neatly compartmentalised. They operate in conjunction with each other, different combinations working together to affect any individual's orientation to learning. Certain influences may take on greater prominence at different times; so any individual's orientation to learning may vary at different times and over time. Here, we focus on the individual influences on teachers' learning (Figure 4.1), although we also refer to school context influences (described in more detail in Chapter 6) and external influences (described in more detail in Chapter 7).

EXPERIENCE

Teachers bring a wealth of experience to their learning. Teachers' individual career patterns, their priorities and their stage in life all influence their desire to learn (Huberman, 1988; Sikes, 1992). Particular

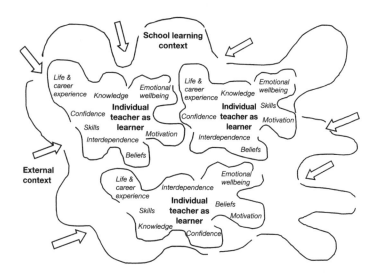

Figure 4.1 Individual influences on teachers as learners

Source: Based on Stoll (1999)

change events occur in people's lives, altering their previous goals, attitudes and behaviours, and leading them towards new learning.

> Think back to your own schooling. How has this influenced your orientations to learning?

BELIEFS

Teachers' perceptions and actions about changing and developing their teaching are influenced by their beliefs. For example, some teachers may resist learning a new reading technique because they believe that teaching reading using this method does not work, based on 25 years of experience using different methods.

EMOTIONS

Teachers' readiness to engage in learning is influenced by their psychological state. Neglecting emotions can close people up to learning, and lead teachers to behave defensively to protect themselves from innovations that they might feel expose their 'inadequacies'. When teachers feel that they and their contributions are valued, their self-esteem is enhanced and trust is built. This leads to greater openness to learning. As a staff development co-ordinator in a Scottish primary school involved in one of our projects commented, 'If staff do not feel valued, they will not want to continue their personal development'.

MOTIVATION

Motivation has been described as the starting point for learning (Biggs and Moore, 1993). For busy and often overworked teachers to devote effort to change and new learning, there has to be a good reason. They need some sort of catalyst or 'urgency' (Earl and Lee, 2000): 'What I'm doing doesn't seem to be working' or 'Here is an alternative way that might improve my practice'. Faced with a new teaching strategy, teachers want to know it is practical and useful – 'relevant to me in my classroom with these pupils'. Teachers also need to feel they have some choice in their learning and that it connects to their work and what interests them. They also need to find a learning experience meaningful to sustain involvement in it (see Table 4.2).

CONFIDENCE

Teachers' confidence that they can make a difference and achieve the desired results influences their orientation to learning. Without confidence in the likelihood of being successful, motivation is insufficient. For example, three-way pupil–parent–teacher conferences require new connections with parents that some teachers might find daunting.

INTERDEPENDENCY

Most humans depend on connections, relationships and social support. While many teachers may express their individuality and choose, at

Table 4.2 Influences on adult motivation for learning

Levels	How motivation operates
i) Success + volition	At the most critical and basic level of positive adult motivation for learning, adults have to experience choice, willingness and success in their learning.
ii) Success + volition + value	The learner doesn't necessarily find the learning activity exciting or enjoyable, but takes it seriously and sees its relevance, finding it meaningful and worthwhile.
iii) Success + volition, value + enjoyment	The highest level of progression, where the adult experiences the learning as pleasurable.

Source: Based on Wlodkowski (1999)

appropriate times, to work and learn alone, many also see the potential of their interaction with and support from others – and know they and their work benefit from collaboration. Indeed, as we have argued, learning is social: teachers learn through interdependency.

INDIVIDUALITY

Teachers bring their own individuality to their learning – personal preferences, approaches, strategies and capabilities for learning, that are affected by their experience and heredity, social and cultural backgrounds. Such factors shape their orientation to learning.

What different kinds of learners do you have on your staff? How does your school use this diversity to support teacher learning?

SCHOOL CONTEXT

Teachers are influenced by the context within which they work. The range of pupils they teach – in terms of ethnic groups, social class, cultural background, age, gender mix, and special educational needs – plays a role in the particular learning needs of teachers. Teachers are also influenced by what goes on in the workplace: relationships; morale; school culture; power and control issues; structures; the school's history; and leadership. We explore the school conditions that best seem to support teacher learning in Chapter 5.

EXTERNAL CONTEXT

Teachers' contextual reality also includes change forces described in Chapter 1, the external community, access to professional learning opportunities, and government reforms as well as 'tone' of policy directives (Stoll, 1999). Teachers' learning may almost be paralysed in the time leading up to an OFSTED inspection, they may find themselves engaged in compulsory training for the National Literacy Strategy, or their school may have been identified as a failing school.

> *Learning is like rowing against the tide. Once you stop doing it, you drift back.*
> Benjamin Britten

Enhancing teacher learning

It is ultimately up to each teacher to take charge of her or his own continuous learning. Given what we know about different ways people learn and issues in teachers' lives influencing readiness for learning, there's no one way for teachers to support, develop and enhance their own learning. Here we offer examples of different ways to engage in learning. In each case, we assume the onus is on individual teachers to take the lead in choosing preferred ways of learning and varying the learning activities they engage in and processes they use to enhance their learning. The likelihood of teachers choosing to engage in continuous learning will be much greater in a school where conditions are in place to support teacher learning (we address these conditions in the following two chapters).

Using an organiser of 'r' words (with one slight cheat), we have selected seven ways in which teachers might move along the learning curve (Figure 4.2), although we know there are others and you may want to come up with some too.

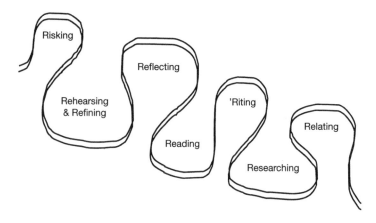

Figure 4.2 The seven 'rs' of teachers' learning curves

Reflecting

In your busy life, how often do you take time to reflect on what you do, particularly when you are doing it? Reflection is central to understanding and development. Here we suggest four kinds.

The first is related to your actions as a teacher. Donald Schön (1983) has distinguished between *reflection-in-action* – the spontaneous decision-making process teachers engage in while they are actively involved in teaching – and *reflection-on-action* – when teachers reflect on their teaching away from (before or after) the actual teaching experience.

When you reflect on your teaching and your pupils' learning in a specific lesson or task, ask yourself the following questions (Ashton *et al.*, 1981). *What were the learners actually doing? What were they learning? How worthwhile was it? What did I/we do? What did I/we learn? What will I/we do next?*

The second is to become *assessment literate* (Stiggins, 1991), taking an inquiry-minded approach to data about your pupils' progress and development. Look for differences between girls and boys, older and younger pupils, pupils from different cultural and social back-grounds, and for differences results for the same pupils in different subjects. If you collect data about pupils' attitudes to school and their self-esteem (see under *Risking*, p. 96), ask questions if pupils appear to do well in Key Stage or GCSE assessments but express concerns about bullying or the difficulty of making friends.

The third kind of reflection is *meta-learning* – learning about your own learning. It is just as important for you as a teacher as for your pupils to understand what helps you to learn, what prevents you from learning, what intelligences, styles and learning preferences you bring to their learning, in what contexts you learn best, whether you learn better alone or with others, and other key considerations. Through understanding your own learning experiences, you can get more out of future learning experiences.

In a useful activity for teacher learners, Watkins and colleagues suggest that Dennison and Kirk's (1990) learning cycle (based on Kolb, 1984) can help people's meta-learning (see Figure 4.3). By asking them to review their experiences of learning, focusing at each stage on their *purpose*, *strategy*, the *effects*, their *feelings* and the *context*, the adult learner can review her or his learning, learn about the learning and apply what they have learnt to their future learning.

Fourth, reflecting includes asking the question '*What's in it for the pupils?*' You need to consider the link between your own learning and that of your pupils, thinking of ways you can monitor the changes in your learning and its impact on your pupils.

Rehearsing and refining

Teaching for understanding is not a simple task. Teachers themselves have to construct their own understanding of what it means. If you try to implement the surface features of teaching for understanding without having a good grasp of the theory itself, you are likely to miss the meaning and the results will be off the mark. You may be faced with the prospect of adopting a whole new way of teaching and casting aside or unlearning much of what you have known and done confidently before. This requires a significant amount of practice to develop your understanding. A classically trained violinist faced with a new piece composed for jazz fiddle is likely to have to practise harder

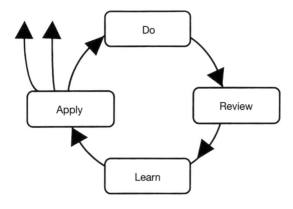

Figure 4.3 Cycle of learning
Source: Dennison and Kirk (1990)

to master the different rhythms and dynamics. An artist like Seurat would have developed his pointillist technique through much trial and error. Many of the artist's drawings and sketches hanging in exhibitions are practice attempts. Similarly, the play at the theatre has gone through a rehearsal period, and that is after the actors and actresses have already devoted significant time and a range of strategies to learning their lines.

Reading

We frequently hear from teachers that they don't have time to read. The same is sometimes true for academics. People who manage to make time, however, often find a wealth of good and stimulating ideas. We know of groups of teachers and whole school staffs who have developed study groups and book clubs. Access to the internet brings opportunities to search for topics of particular interest and literature on any number of learning and teaching challenges. Many universities and other organisations provide concise research summaries, and there is an increasing number of professional journals. Increasingly, these journals contain articles written by teachers.

Co-operative group reading task (Jigsaw activity)

You'll need at least an hour for this if you do the whole activity, but it's worth the time.

1. Pick a topic e.g. action research, using questions, assessment for learning, etc.
2. Find four short articles or chapters about the topic and number them 1–4.
3. Decide what questions you want to answer through your reading and tell colleagues the questions before they start reading. Alternatively, ask them to come up with questions.
4. Divide the whole group into 'home' groups of four and give one of the four pieces of writing to each person in the group to read ready to discuss with colleagues (15–20 minutes – deep reading isn't necessary).
5. Create 'expert' groups of three or four people, all of whom have read the same piece, to discuss their reading and how it helps them answer the questions (15 minutes).
6. Return to 'home' groups, tell each other about your four readings and discuss the questions together (20–30 minutes).
7. Summarise discussions as a whole group (10 minutes).

You can omit stage 5, but in our experience the subsequent discussion is less rich.

'Riting

All of us write a lot, but we can all remember when we found writing very difficult. As academic supervisors of students doing higher degrees, we have also seen tremendous development in students' writing over time. Our advice to anyone who feels anxious about putting thoughts and experiences on paper is 'just do it'. Joellen Killion (1999), an experienced American staff developer, sees journal writing as a powerful form of learning because when an idea is transferred into language, the mind has to process and clarify the idea. She also points out that it is an inexpensive form of learning, is easily transportable, can be personalised to meet individual learners' needs, and can be accessed whenever the learner wishes. 'Journal writing . . . becomes a place for learners to record observations, toy with various perspectives, analyze their own practice, interpret their understanding of topics, keep records, make comments, or reconstruct experiences' (Killion, 1999).

Staff of one inner-city primary school involved in a project with one of us focused on improving pupils' writing. They decided to keep journals of their experiences and issues they were facing. The journals were left in the staff room where colleagues could read them and write responses or offer suggestions.

Writing can help you to see how much you have achieved and where you might develop further. A key part of any kind of performance appraisal is reflecting beforehand when writing about the previous year. It's easy to remember all the things you haven't done and things that didn't go the way you planned, but it's valuable to write about your successes and the reasons for them, as well as what you learnt about yourself and your work in the last year.

Professional development portfolios are increasingly used. They will be most useful if used to reflect and write about what prior learning means for future learning and development. A middle years teacher in Connecticut wrote about her experience of building teacher portfolios (Van Wagenen and Hibbard, 1998). It took three years and the support of a reflective journal to learn to write reflective essays, showing what she had learnt: 'In our early attempts, we focused mostly on the question "What did we do?" As we looked back on those early essays, we realized that we needed to address two more questions: "So what did we learn?" and "Now what will we do?" Now three phrases form the structure of every Connecticut Educator's Collaborative Portfolio: What? So What? Now What?' (See parallels between these questions and those asked in the *Reflecting* section, p. 88–89.)

Researching

Many teachers are now researching aspects of their classroom and school practice. This is an exciting development, with teachers collecting a range of forms of evidence about more successful learning and teaching strategies and conditions that support them within their own contexts. As Marion Dadds (1995) notes, in following one teacher engaged in action research:

> Observation work had been a valuable part of the research and learning process. More looking had led to more seeing. More seeing had led to more understanding and changes in professional perception. 'I've learnt observation techniques', she said. 'I now stand back and observe the children, myself and other staff. I see more and I understand more'.

Dimmock (2000) usefully draws attention to the distinction between 'best practice' and 'informed practice'. He argues that the former implies there is only one best way of learning, teaching, or indeed, managing. 'Informed practice', he suggests, indicates that teachers can usefully draw on evidence, bearing in mind that this evidence was collected in a different situation. What is most important is that researching your practice can help inform you about 'what seems to promote better learning with my/our pupils at this time'.

Here are some questions you might ask when starting a research enquiry:

- What is your topic of inquiry? What is the 'problem' you want to understand more about in your learning/teaching/classroom/department/school?
- Why have you selected this topic/this problem?
- What evidence do you have to show this needs to be addressed?
- What literature/documentation/government reports can you find to support your rationale for choosing this area of focus?
- How do you plan to research the issue?
- Why do you intend to do it that way?
- How will you work with others in carrying out this inquiry?
- What problems do you foresee in carrying out your inquiry?
- How do you anticipate dealing with them?
- How will you analyse what you have done?
- How will you evaluate your work? What evidence will you need to collect now?

After you have completed the study and to help you with your analysis and reflection:

- What did you do?
- Why?
- What went well? Why, and how do you know?
- What didn't go so well? Why, and how do you know?
- Has it benefited the pupils' learning? How do you know? What is your evidence?
- What did you learn from this?
- How can you apply what you have learned to future situations?
- How has your enquiry helped improve your practice?
- If you were doing it again, how might you do it differently next time?

Research can be an individual activity but it can also be a collaborative activity, with pairs or groups of teachers working together exploring issues from a variety of angles: for example, does independent learning mean the same thing to pupils, teachers and parents? It is to relating as a form of teacher learning that we now turn.

> . . . action research can enable teachers to ask critical questions about their practice and to undertake systematic means of inquiry in order to understand or improve their practice.
>
> Sachs (2000)

Relating

Colleagues can help deepen teachers' learning. This 'r' is about collegiality as a central feature of teacher learning and development, emphasising mutual sharing and assistance, a whole-school development orientation and what Judith Warren Little (1990) described as *joint work* and found to be the most powerful form of professional development. Examples include team teaching, mentoring, collaborative action research, peer coaching, joint planning and mutual observation and feedback. As a secondary school improvement team member involved in one of our improvement projects commented:

> . . . our main aim is to change our classroom practice supported by our colleagues, and as a major part of that we want to be able to observe each other in the classroom, to be able to have someone

who can be what we are calling a 'reflective friend' to whom you can talk afterwards about the things that went well, the things that didn't go so well.

One of us evaluated a primary-school restructuring initiative in Geneva. Of three aims, one was developing collegiality within schools in a system where individualism is the norm. This was incredibly challenging, but some teachers were more successful than others, developing learning and teaching activities involving pupils of all ages, and bringing teams of teachers from across the school together to plan, implement, manage and evaluate these.

Collaborative planning can be frustrating but ultimately rewarding, as some middle years teachers told one of us: 'there were six of us . . . six people who are real individuals, with very distinctive styles in teaching, and there were a lot of arguments . . . and yet at the end of the sessions, we were proud of the results and we weren't afraid of differing opinions.'

Lipton and Wellman with Humbard (2001) describe mentors as 'powerful models for novice teachers as they describe their own learning goals and help protégés craft meaningful challenges of their own'. New teacher and student teacher mentoring by more experienced colleagues offers benefits to both partners, with the new or novice teacher acting as a fresh pair of eyes on the mentor's classroom practice. Peer coaching relationships can be equally useful, involving a more equal partnership in terms of length of experience or interest.

Wragg (1999) describes reciprocal pair work – two teachers pairing up to study and observe each other – as 'a rich form of professional development'. He suggests a range of tasks worth investigating. One example is two infant schools looking at how they hear children read, and monitoring progress to see if any changes they make – without 'teaching to the test' – lead to an improvement in children's reading ability. Another example is two secondary science teachers sitting in on each other's laboratory sessions to watch small groups during experimental work, noting how effectively they learn the topic and how harmoniously they work together. He suggests that interviewing some pupils after the lesson might also be beneficial to see how well they understand what they have been doing.

Being part of school improvement teams or cadres may not be considered a form of teacher learning. However, being involved in creative problem solving about how to develop your school, bring about positive change, stimulate colleagues' interest in and commitment to such initiatives, and resolve inevitable difficulties as they occur, can be profoundly important learning experiences. As one teacher member of a school improvement cadre in a secondary school participating in the IQEA (Improving the Quality of Education for All) network told one of us: 'At first we thought the university team would come and tell us . . . we were put into a tricky situation. We had to find our own capacity. They taught us we have the inner capacity to change things and expertise at [school name] . . . We are change agents. I've changed. My reflective powers have increased. I'm consciously competent' (Wikeley *et al.*, 2000).

Networking provides an arena for developing collegial relationships beyond school. Teacher subject groups, teachers' centres, school development team networks and Education Action Zones are only a few examples. Academics in higher education institutions and LEAs have developed projects with built-in networking opportunities for putting practitioners in touch with each other, to share and debate ideas, resolve issues and have access to current research (for example Hopkins *et al.*, 1994; Stoll and Fink, 1996; Southworth and Lincoln, 1999; Ethos Network, www.ethosnet.co.uk). Rapidly expanding opportunities also exist for teacher networking through ICT, as schools become connected to the internet, set up websites and link up with each other. Such connections may be no substitute for face-to-face interaction, but they certainly combat isolation and lack of access.

Risking

This 'r' is as much about the mindset you bring to your learning as particular forms of learning. It could apply, for example, to writing and peer observation if you've never done them before. Trying out new strategies and ideas inevitably means taking a risk, but it's important to feel safe to do so. Michael Fullan and Andy Hargreaves (1992) suggest trying out new practices on a small scale, but also attempting to be the first to try out new forms of professionalism. If you invite colleagues to observe you teaching and give feedback, you want to be comfortable if things don't quite go the way you had intended. As another teacher in the 'reflective friends' school commented: 'A reflective friend is someone who you can feel safe with, you can describe things to, and hopefully they're going to give you some sort of support or criticism which is going to allow you to develop.'

> Make just a ripple, come on be brave.
> This time a ripple, next time a wave.
> Sometimes you have to start small, climbing the tiniest wall,
> Maybe you're going to fall, but it's better than not starting at all.
> Stephen Sondheim, 'Everybody Says Don't'
> (from *Anyone Can Whistle*)

Letting pupils become partners in the learning process can be even more risky. In a project one of us was involved in, focusing on pupils' learning in the middle years (Years 5–8), just over a third of the secondary teachers we surveyed agreed with the statement 'Teachers see pupils as partners in the learning process' (81 percent, however, felt this was important) (Muschamp *et al.*, 2001). Increasingly, schools are using pupil surveys to tap into their pupils' attitudes about schooling. It takes a risk to ask pupils what they think about their schooling. As we have noted elsewhere in this book, Michael Fielding (2001b) suggests teachers need to be even more radical, involving pupils as researchers, rather than just a source of data, active respondents or co-researchers.

This task can be done individually, in a small group, or by a whole staff.

For each of the 'r's, answer the following questions:
What are some examples of me/us doing this?
What did I/we gain from engaging in these activities?
What difficulties did I/we experience?
What does it tell me/us about my/our own learning?

Now answer some general questions:
Which appear to be particularly effective modes of learning for me/us?
Which modes are underused/underdeveloped?
How can I/we enhance my/our own learning?

. . . And what about time?

Linda Darling-Hammond (1999) argues that: 'the time teachers spend with each other and with other knowledgeable educators – engaged in thinking about teaching and learning – is just as important to students' opportunities to learn as the time teachers spend in direct facilitation of learning'. There's no getting away from it: learning and change take time, and need investment of time. There is growing evidence from reform efforts around the world that lack of time is the critical block to teacher learning and school improvement (Tye, 2000; Hargreaves *et al.*, 2000). There's a tension here: extended within-school time away from pupils means potential disruption to their learning. But, does learning always have to take place away from pupils? Perhaps 15 minutes of silent reading could mean the teacher also has 15 minutes for silent reading. Alternatively, the head might take one class while that teacher observes a colleague, or two teachers may combine classes for a session to team teach something planned together. A supply teacher might rotate around classes, rather than working with one group of pupils or teaching a particular subject all day. Another idea is having an advisory teacher or literacy co-ordinator working in teachers' classrooms with them. Sometimes, however, you just need time away from school to learn something new, before coming back, trying it out and practising it. This may mean short-term 'pain', being away from school, but can lead to long-term gain, as long as time, ongoing support and coaching opportunities are available when you get back.

> For teachers, going to school must be as much about learning as it is about teaching. They must have time each day to learn, plan lessons, critique student work, and support improvement as members of learning teams . . . Staff development cannot be something educators do only on specified days in the school calendar. It must be part of every educator's daily work schedule.
>
> Hirsch (2001)

While more difficult and perhaps less palatable, it may be necessary to rethink traditional school organisations, especially in secondary schools – 'one teacher–one class' teacher deployment – in order to find the time required to promote teacher and therefore pupil learning

(Hargreaves, 1994; Stoll and Fink, 1996; Adelman and Walking-Eagle, 1997; Dimmock, 2000).

Time is not a new concept in education. Nevertheless, the speed of reforms and the relatively rigid structures of schools put time at the forefront for teachers. Time in schools is not only scheduled, it is rhythmic and cyclical, and it is experienced differently depending on the situation. Since the rhythms of schools and teachers are interlocked, it is important to try to maximise the quality time that is available for teachers not only to teach well but to learn well. The standard organisation of schools with classes lasting a set number of minutes and 25–30 pupils in a room with a single teacher severely limits the ways in which time can be allocated and used. Over the years we have observed many innovative strategies for changing the nature and the experience of time in schools. In one secondary school, the teachers of older pupils had a half-day each term to work together on curriculum development and professional development. The headteacher and deputy heads worked with a committee of pupils to develop a programme for the pupils that they organised, led and monitored. This programme included a performance and lecture delivered by a successful rock band who had attended local schools. The follow-up discussion was heated and challenging for pupils and focused on the skills and wisdom that professional musicians needed to survive – skills like accounting, public speaking, identifying when they were being manipulated, staying fit and healthy. The only regret on the part of the teachers was that they missed the pupil-run programmes.

> Consider the following questions in relation to your school:
> Do teachers have special time for planning, individually and together?
> Is teaching time considered 'sacred'?
> Where is the time for teachers to learn new skills and explore new ideas?

What's in it for schools?

The development of schools as learning communities depends on teacher learning. In learning-enriched schools (Rosenholtz, 1989) teachers

> *Probably nothing within a school has more impact on students in terms of skills development, self-confidence, or classroom behavior than the personal and professional growth of their teachers.*
>
> Barth (1990)

see their own learning as cumulative and developmental. They also believe that learning to teach is a lifelong pursuit. As one commented, 'You never stop learning. Our school has many different levels achievement-wise. And students also differ culturally. It's important to learn how to teach something in as many ways as possible to reach all these students. I'm always on the search for new ideas.'

Susan Rosenholtz also found links between greater opportunities for teachers to learn and increased reading and maths performance gains among these teachers' students. Teacher learning leads to a sense of confidence about one's practice, especially when teachers see the differences in their pupils' learning, development and achievement.

Earlier, we introduced the concept of flow in which the individual is so completely absorbed in a task that (s)he is totally unselfconscious and engaged in 'the pleasure of the learning and the doing' (Csikszentmihalyi, 1990). When people are in flow they are self-motivated, self-directed professionals, enjoying the challenge of learning curves. 'Flow', however, only occurs when people perceive their skills and learning as sufficient to meet the demands of the task. This is a delicate balance between challenge and skill. Too much challenge creates anxiety, and skill without challenge promotes boredom. Leaders can promote 'flow' by creating the conditions in schools that balance skill and challenge. In Chapter 5 we turn to leaders' learning as a prerequisite to both teachers' and pupils' learning.

Further reading and network sources

Learning about Learning is a great set of resources for supporting effective learning of teachers and pupils. Chris Watkins, Eileen Carnell, Caroline Lodge, Caroline Whalley and Patsy Wagner have drawn on their combined experience of working in a range of roles in schools, LEAs and universities, in connection with *napce* to produce thought-provoking and challenging tasks and follow-up reading (www.napce.org.uk).

Staff developers and leaders will find special appeal in Raymond Wlodkowski's book, *Enhancing Adult Motivation to Learn*, which offers many useful insights on motivating adults and some practical tools.

What's Worth Fighting For in Your School by Michael Fullan and Andy Hargreaves has been on our list of good reads for several years. The authors' concept of interactive professionalism elaborates what we mean when we talk about new professionalism. We know many people in schools who have read and enjoyed this book.

We can't ignore Daniel Goleman's *Emotional Intelligence*. It has had a major impact on educators in many countries and has set many people thinking about a neglected topic.

Chris Day's *Developing Teachers: The Challenges of Lifelong Learning* is a serious read, containing important insights gained from years of experience researching teacher development. It comprehensively examines teacher professionalism and continuing professional development, analysing these within the contexts in which they occur, and discussing the possibilities of networks, partnerships and the role of teachers in a learning society.

Assessment Literacy for Wise Decisions, by Sue Swaffield and Pete Dudley, is a valuable publication, commissioned by the Association of Teachers and Lecturers (ATL), that explains assessment issues clearly, and recommends useful websites and books.

The journal *Professional Development Today* publishes short, readable articles on key professional development issues. The National Staff Development Council in the US (www.nsdc.org) has a journal, *Journal of Staff Development*, with plenty of practical ideas. If they ask you who recommended them, tell them it was us!

MirandaNet (www.mirandanet.ac.uk) is an example of a network aimed at using multimedia to support the development of international learning communities and enrich lifelong learning.

5 Leadership for learning and learning for leadership for learning

Throughout this book we have made the case that as educators we must keep our eyes firmly fixed on the purpose of schooling: learning – *learning to know, to do, to live together* and *to be*. In the midst of a plethora of policy mandates, accountability measures and public pressures, this is often a daunting challenge, especially for school leaders. Headteachers, for example, see the world of education and change in very different ways. One American study concluded that principals handled these twin pressures in one of three ways (Tye, 2000). By limiting themselves to managing the school and responding only to directives from higher sources, some leaders adopted a *coping* strategy. Conversely, others were aware of new trends and indiscriminately set goals for their school. This *diffusion* strategy occurs in what Bryk and his colleagues (1998) describe as 'Christmas tree schools'. The leaders in such schools just keep hanging new ideas and innovations on top of old ones in the hope that a few will survive. The third leaders' orientation is *goal-focused* in which the leaders and staff select a few reasonable goals, establish priorities and ignore or manage other pressures. Barbara Tye (2000) suggests that such leaders have an intuitive sense for what is important (and what is not), combined with a willingness to risk displeasing those 'higher up' by declining to carry out some of their demands.

If, as we have suggested, the agenda for schools is about learning and time, it is important to concentrate on improved learning for everyone in schools. To achieve superior learning we must focus on the core leadership role of leadership for learning. We do this intentionally in this chapter, while recognising that this is not the whole story for school leaders.

In any organisation, schools included, leadership is not invested in only one person. Peter Senge and his colleagues (1999) identify three types of leaders in an organisation: executive leaders, line leaders and network leaders.

- *Executive leaders* – heads, deputies and other senior managers – possessing the formal and legitimated power of the organisation.
- *Line leaders* – subject and Key Stage co-ordinators, heads of departments and heads of years – possessing the power delegated to them by the executive leaders, and holding formal power over those who report to them.
- *Informal or 'network' leaders* – with the potential and flexibility to cross organisational boundaries and promote whole-school initiatives, often more effectively than formal leaders.

Both executive and line leaders are frequently constrained by the boundaries of their roles. Formal leaders, therefore, must tap into the school's informal networks to promote 'network' leadership. We believe the nature of leadership and the learnings we describe in this chapter are equally appropriate to both formal and informal leaders. They provide a model for formal leaders to encourage the kind of 'network' leaders and 'distributive' leadership in a school that promotes improved pupils' learning (see Southworth and Conner, 1999; Riley and Louis, 2000; Moon *et al.*, 2000). What, then, are these necessary learnings?

Learnings for leaders for learning

We don't intend to provide a simple laundry list of technical competencies. Leadership for learning isn't a destination with fixed coordinates on a compass, but a journey with plenty of detours and even some dead ends. Effective educational leaders are continuously open to new learning because the journey keeps changing. Their maps are complex and can be confusing. What we believe leaders require for this journey is a set of seven interrelated learnings that look at school leadership in a holistic rather than a reductionist way. These learnings can be deepened, elaborated, nurtured, abandoned, and connected and related to other learnings as the journey progresses.

Understanding learning

It isn't only teachers who need to understand the learning process. To promote learning and support others' learning, leaders need to have a deep, current and critical understanding of the learning process. For example, the University of Chicago's Center for School Improvement has found in more than 12 years of working with urban elementary schools on whole-school literacy development that little changes unless the principal is fully on board (Bryk *et al.*, 1996). The key to ensuring principals' commitment has been helping them develop their own literacy expertise sufficiently to support implementation of literacy development in their schools. At network meetings principals collectively analyse videotapes of classroom teaching, revisiting practices that constitute good pedagogy. Subject leaders are also critical to improvement (Busher and Harris with Wise, 2000). While leaders may not have in-depth knowledge of the content of the entire curriculum for which they may be responsible, they should possess such rich insights into the learning–teaching process that they can determine effective practice among their colleagues and provide appropriate and timely assistance to them. Leaders should see themselves as advocates for pupils, and only leaders with a deep understanding of the learning process can fulfil this role effectively. Moreover, leaders require a deep understanding of how adults learn, as described in the previous chapter, to enable them to provide support for teachers' learning to support pupils' learning.

Making connections

There is an old story of four blind men encountering an elephant and trying to determine what it is. One, feeling a leg, declares the unknown object to be a tree. A second, feeling a tusk, identifies the object as a spear and a third, holding onto a squirming trunk, decides it must be a snake. The fourth, touching an ear, announces that they have found a fan. Developing improvement strategies in a school can often turn into this kind of process. Participants identify the school's needs and directions from their unique perceptions. It is the leaders' role to see the entire organisation and help stakeholders to view the school in a holistic way. Leaders provide coherence and make connections so that others can see the interrelationships and interconnections between the many things happening in a school. The development of a school-wide perspective is an important 'learning' to promote positive change. To promote a holistic view, leaders must learn how to look at change in multi-dimensional ways – to look at change through multiple frames or lenses (Bolman and Deal, 1997; Louis *et al.*, 1999; Fink, 2000). We discuss this in more detail in Chapter 6.

Schools for the most part are structured along mechanistic lines. Pupils are grouped into classes, years and subjects. Teachers in schools are often separated by physical location, subject areas or Key Stages and departments. Parents have access to their children's schools through formalised structures such as parents' nights and governors' meetings. In many ways, the existing structures of time, space, roles and responsibilities divide key school stakeholders into their parts rather than create the unity that makes for powerful learning communities. Leaders need to learn how to make connections among all the people comprising the school community – pupils, teachers, support staff, parents – and between the school and the larger community.

Futures thinking

Successful leaders must also learn how to connect the past, the present and the future. A consistent theme of both school effectiveness and school improvement literatures is the need for shared goals and a shared sense of direction. Leaders' awareness and understanding of forces influencing the life of a school are crucial to shaping this shared sense of vision. If you don't know where you are going, any place will do. Leaders who can mould a school's vision in productive and inspiring ways look at the world around them ecologically. They attempt to understand the dynamics of the social forces described in Chapter 1 – and the many other compelling and complex social forces shaping our world – and relate them to the life of their school. Leaders are also aware of shifting currents of local political, social and economic forces and help staff to understand the connections between and among global, national and local forces. Not only are leaders problem-solvers, they must be active problem seekers (Louis and Miles, 1990). Anticipating the future enables leaders to help colleagues act strategically rather than randomly as they journey into the future (Davies and Ellison, 1999). Experience is also important in futures thinking.

It provides a useful grounding in reality and understanding of the complexities of change. Leadership and the ability to look 'Janus-like' (Kouzes and Posner, 2000) – both forward and backward at the same time – develop in large measure from experience, often from making mistakes.

Since schools are labour-intensive organisations, strategies to recruit, induct and develop staff are crucial parts of futures thinking. Successful schools build a critical mass of formal and informal leaders who influence more reluctant colleagues to move forward on agreed-upon changes. Innovative and successful schools tend to produce leaders who are often promoted to other settings. Leaders who intend to perpetuate the best of a school's culture have a plan to replace these key people. Many innovative settings lose momentum because of the failure of their leaders to plan for succession – ensuring there are new leaders to take over after key staff members have left (Fink, 2000).

Contextual knowledge

Successful leaders make further connections by developing firm knowledge and understanding of their context. Context relates to the particular situation, background or environment in which something is happening. Two of us have described five different school contexts – *moving, cruising, struggling, strolling* and *sinking* (Stoll and Fink, 1996). Keeping a *moving* school moving or 'jump-starting' a *cruising* school are different challenges from leading *sinking* and *struggling* schools because of their different contexts (Stoll and Myers, 1998). The idea of 'one size fits all', whether the topic is curriculum, pedagogy, assessment or leadership, is nonsense, because it fails to account for the uniqueness of individuals and contexts. Leaders must have strategies for analysing their contexts and responding to their unique characteristics. In addition to knowing about pupil achievement in total, they need to know how various sub-groups in the school are doing, for example, how girls compare to boys. Context-aware leaders know how the pupils, parents and staff feel about the school. They understand the deeper social context in which their school operates. We develop this idea further in Chapter 6.

Critical thinking

What differentiates effective leaders and ineffective leaders is the quality of their judgements: whether their decisions work for the pupils in the long term. The greatest challenge for educators, of course, is to determine whether their judgements are 'wise' because the results sometimes do not show up for years. Education is for a lifetime, even if policy makers want demonstrations of success in the short term. Ken Leithwood and colleagues (1999) refer to this area of learning as leaders' 'problem-solving processes' – leaders' responses to unique and organisational circumstances or problems they face.

There are plenty of people with answers, but few with the wisdom and judgement to ask the right questions (Secretan, 1996). A significant part of a formal leader's job is to act as a gatekeeper, to ask the right questions, to know what initiatives to support, what to oppose, and what to subvert.

Political acumen

School leaders must represent the interests of their school to the governing body, the community, the LEA, OFSTED inspectors and the DfES. Politics is about power and influence, and to ignore political issues or consider that political activity is unworthy of a leader is to leave the school, its staff, pupils and parents vulnerable to competing social forces.

At micro levels, schools are filled with groups and individuals with different interests, and that occasionally leads to conflict. Leaders use political methods, such as negotiation and coalition building to move schools towards agreed-upon goals. Blase (1998) talks about positive politics and discriminates between 'power over' and 'power with', suggesting that leaders who are prepared to share power and influence 'with' other groups and agencies can create positive politics. Leaders need to learn 'bridge-building' strategies at both macro and micro political levels.

Emotional understanding

Leadership is about getting ordinary people to do extraordinary things. More contemporary notions of leadership suggest that 'what people find rewarding gets done'. Sergiovanni (1992) goes further, arguing that that which is seen as 'good' and morally purposeful gets done. To create an environment in which teachers find 'flow' (Csikszentmihalyi, 1990) requires leaders with emotional understanding. In Chapter 4 we discussed the concept of emotional understanding between teachers and pupils; we now extend it to include leaders and their colleagues. Leaders with emotional understanding learn to read the emotional responses of those around them and create emotional engagements and bonds with and among those with whom they interact. Andy Hargreaves (1998) explains that the emotions of educational change most commonly addressed are ones helping to defuse so-called 'resistance' to change like trust, support, involvement, commitment to teamwork and willingness to experiment. Leaders with emotional understanding do, however, lead their colleagues into uncharted territory on the change journey through the 'impassioned and critical engagement or critique' of ideas, purposes and practices.

This discussion suggests a rather complex jigsaw puzzle that leaders need to put together carefully and cleverly. How can leaders assemble this puzzle? We now turn to discuss how learners enhance their own learning and that of others.

> In a situation where the past is all too familiar, the future untried and the present uncertain, a clearly-defined understanding of what makes for effective leadership is of the utmost importance. Learning how to use that understanding to make more effective leaders is essential.
>
> MacBeath, Moos and Riley (1998)

Enhancing leaders' own learning

Leadership for a changing educational environment requires a different face: an alternative to prevailing models. Previously, two of us suggested an approach that reflects the rational and non-rational, the predictable and unpredictable aspects of leadership in schools, and recognises school leaders' multiple roles. Moreover, this model of leadership advocates a 'doing with' people as opposed to a 'doing to'. It is a view that captures both the personal and professional aspects of school leadership and blends emotional understanding with rational management strategies.

We called this approach 'invitational leadership' (Stoll and Fink, 1996). Others use terms such as 'servant leadership' (Greenleaf, 1977), 'moral leadership' (Sergiovanni, 1992), 'stewardship leadership' (Block, 1993) and 'values-led contingency leadership' (Day *et al.*, 2000) to communicate similar ideas. Regardless of the label, leadership is more than a technical activity intended to implement someone else's change agenda. School leadership is a profoundly moral, ethical and emotional activity designed to encourage a school's staff to build and act on a shared and evolving vision of enhanced educational experiences for pupils. Such leadership should be dynamic, holistic, flexible and humane, but also purposeful and firm where necessary. In the invitational leadership model, leaders invite themselves and others both personally and professionally. Attending to personal and professional growth, and building supportive and respectful relationships with others, are prerequisites to developing the professional learnings we have described.

Inviting yourself personally

Organisational change requires change in the people who make up the organisation. One person can't change another. To suggest such an idea is to deny individual 'free will'. Leaders can create environments or contexts in which others may 'choose' to change their practices, but a leader can't make a person change. This is terrible news for those who feel that directives to leaders will promote positive change down the line. The only people leaders can directly change are themselves. We've listed a few learnings necessary to invite oneself personally, again using an organiser of words beginning with 'r', with a few related activities. Simply stated, if you haven't invited yourself, how can you invite others to be better than they are?

Regenerating

List the various roles you play in life – for example: leader, partner, parent, community participant, etc. Organise these roles in priority from the most to the least important. Using 100 per cent to indicate your waking hours in a week, allocate a percentage of your weekly time to each of these roles. Do you spend your time according to your priorities? Is your life in balance? Do you invite yourself personally?

Similarly, list the ways in which you prepare yourself for leadership by inviting yourself physically, intellectually, socially/emotionally, and spiritually. Is your life in balance? Are you a centred person?

Recognising

An important personal invitation is to examine one's personal paradigm or mental model of how the world works. Ask yourself: 'What do I do?' 'How did I come to behave in these ways?' 'What are the beliefs that direct my behaviours?' 'How do others respond to my behaviour?' 'How might I change?'

Reclaiming

In Chapter 1 we described the two hungers: the lesser hunger and the greater hunger. Leadership involves reclaiming the high ground and inspiring others through a well-defined idea of moral purpose. 'Reclaiming' requires each leader to look in a mirror and say: 'What do I stand for?' 'What is it that is inviolate?' 'What's my attitude in this situation?' Ask yourself, if 'push came to shove' what behaviours of others would cause you to resign?

In a session with a group of primary heads, asking for more 'r' examples for inviting yourself personally, one of us was informed that 'retail therapy' works wonders! You might want to think of other 'r's.

Inviting yourself professionally

Teachers want to have confidence that leaders know where they are going and have some idea of how to get there. To this end, leaders who succeed assume responsibility for their own professional growth. Invitational leaders invite themselves professionally. We have seven more 'r's – reading and 'riting, relating, reflecting, researching and risking.

> *Learning to learn is the lifelong shadow of learning itself.*
> Claxton (1999)

In a leadership group, list activities that would contribute to leaders' professional learning under each heading. We have given a few examples to get you started.

Reading

List books or articles you have read recently that you believe contributed to your learning as a leader and that you would recommend to your colleagues.

'Riting

Write a 'thought piece' on a topic of interest to you and your colleagues for inclusion in a staff newsletter.

Rehearsing

If you need to return a difficult phone call from a parent or the media, muster as much evidence or information related to the issue as you can and find someone you trust on whom to practise your response before returning the call. Similarly, if you have an important presentation to make to colleagues, governors or the community, try it out on a critical friend or coach (see Chapter 7).

Relating

Online networking helps create communities that can keep in touch. There is also evidence that online discussion groups can promote leaders' 'emotional engagement with learning, development of a critical perspective, movement beyond self and development of agency' (Robertson and Webber, 2000). The next time you go to a conference or a professional activity, develop a small network of colleagues around the topic of the conference or professional activity. Start an e-mail list of people with expertise in areas that interest you. Write to them periodically for advice.

Reflecting

Ask colleagues to list those activities that they think you as a leader should: continue; stop; start. Ask a person that both you and the staff trust to collate the responses then use the results to 'reflect' on your activities as a leader.

Researching

To explore the extent to which your school values learning, you might carry out interviews with groups (four to eight people in each) from across your school community: pupils, teachers, support staff, parents, etc. The key is to ask the same question of each group and then compare and contrast across the groups. For example, you might ask: Do pupils in this school try their best to do well? Do teachers in this school expect and encourage pupils to do their best?

Risking

Learning involves taking risks to try something new. Identify a project that you think will have high pay-off for your school or area of responsibility. Determine the 'driving' or supportive forces that will help you to achieve your goals. List the 'inhibiting' forces. Develop a plan to enhance the driving forces and to remove the inhibiting forces. Make sure you cover yourself politically.

Enhancing others' learning

Leaders need to create the conditions in which the learning of all staff and pupils will prosper. This means inviting others both personally and professionally.

> *. . . it is leaders' role as capacity builder that is fundamental to learning in a complex, changing world.*
> Stoll, Bolam and Collarbone (2002)

Inviting others personally

In an information society, people carry their intellectual capital between their ears. In past times human capital meant sacrificing one's humanity to become part of a larger machine-like organisation. Humans were but another replaceable part of the larger mechanism. Management methods of predictability and control were probably necessary to get people to conform to the dictates of management and to perform routine and repetitive jobs. In an information-based society, however, instrumental images of people are not only dehumanising and ethically reprehensible, but also unproductive and wasteful. Leaders, especially in labour-intensive places like schools, need to relate to colleagues on a personal level, and set in place the personal conditions that will nourish and nurture professional learning.

Susan Rosenholtz's (1989) study *Teachers' Workplace* confirms that workplace conditions actually shape teachers' cognitions about their own learning and the learning of their colleagues. A question Rosenholtz asked teachers was 'How long does it take to learn to teach?' In schools with organisational conditions promoting continuous opportunities for development – *learning-enriched* schools – she found most teachers viewed learning to teach as cumulative and developmental, a lifelong endeavour. In contrast, only a small minority of teachers in *learning-impoverished* schools – where conditions didn't support continuous learning – viewed learning and learning to teach in this way. Instead, she wrote, 'most emphasize a terminal view, perceiving that one acquires teaching skills after a finite and surprisingly few number of years'.

As Seymour Sarason (1990) has articulated so clearly, 'It is virtually impossible to create and sustain over time conditions for productive learning for students when they do not exist for teachers'. From our own and others' research and experience, here is our summary of favourable school conditions that successful leaders promote.

Create a community spirit

A common workshop activity we use is to ask participants to use a metaphor to describe their organisation. We get descriptions like a 'family', a 'team', a 'herd', 'lemmings' an 'orchestra' to mention just a few. The one that we think describes learning communities most accurately is that of a 'jazz ensemble'. In such a group, each person's individuality is respected, each individual's talents are allowed to feature, and plenty of experimentation and improvisation takes place as the group begins to come together to produce its music. Musical scores exist and guide the direction of the piece but participants are not limited to the printed page. The leader creates an environment of safety, encouragement and mutual trust that sustains the group's community spirit over time. A top-flight jazz group can perform at a high level even when the leader is not present because of its internal cohesion and trust. Invitational leaders in schools encourage this respect, mutuality and self-sufficiency among staff members. They honour the uniqueness of each group member and use their strengths and try to modify their weaknesses to optimise the ultimate outcome – learning for pupils. They also support teaching with appropriate resources as an important competency to maintain group harmony and efficacy over time (Smith and Andrews, 1989). Resources mean more than just materials. They include, for example, time, space, use of support staff, counselling, advice and encouragement.

The result of such leadership is a *moving school*, populated with colleagues committed to learning, learning together, and who share a belief that learning should be valued for its own sake and for others' well-being and development. To this end effective leaders can create community spirit by involving teachers in overall decisions about the school's direction and continuing professional development, and attend to individuals' development as well as that of the school as a whole. The process of decision-making itself may be instructive as teachers reflect on ideas and strategies that will enhance learning and teaching.

Relate to others on a personal level

The essence of the educational enterprise is its essential humanity. We are not in the business of making cars or selling insurance or constructing buildings. Our job is to promote pupils' learning. To do this, we invite others personally to see themselves as able, worthwhile and valuable. William Glasser (1997), an American psychologist, says we have four basic human needs – to care and be cared for, to have some power over our circumstances, to have hope, and to have fun. Leaders who invite others personally build the kind of interpersonal relationships that attend to these basic needs by paying attention to teachers' emotional needs and providing emotional support, especially when they feel insecure or vulnerable. Such leaders build supportive relationships, create a climate in which staff members experience a sense of belonging, and provide avenues for the expression of feelings. As one secondary teacher commented:

> *Our deputy is the best I've ever worked with. She's great. She follows up on absolutely everything. She's very firm and yet she has the nicest way with the kids. She always . . . asks how they're doing first; asks them a nice question, and then right to the point but in a very kind, very fair way. I'm impressed with her. I wish I had her ability to do that.*

Provide opportunities for creativity and imagination to flourish

Invitational leaders dare to give of themselves to release the energy and the creativity of others. Hargreaves (1998) explains this notion of releasing people's energies:

> The ability and desire to exceed expectations springs from discretionary commitment – from teachers being prepared to work above and beyond the official call of duty, entirely of their own volition. A leader who is an effective staff developer wants and knows how to create the conditions in which teachers possess that discretionary commitment.

It is only within an environment in which the staff member feels safe and encouraged to try something new, to think 'outside the box', to fail and to try again, that creativity can flourish. By encouraging, publicising and rewarding innovative behaviour, leaders can foster a climate of creativity and imagination. A former colleague of one of us captured this idea well when she described an interaction with one of her leaders this way:

> *I appreciated him more after the fact than at the time. In retrospect when I look back probably one of the things that made him a good leader was that he could talk about what you had done. He would remember and come back a couple of weeks later and say, 'How did such and such work out?' and I would say it was either great or it 'bombed'. If it bombed, he would say, 'Did all of it bomb or did only part of it bomb? Do you have to change it all?' It became a questioning routine so that it got you thinking again as to the*

evaluation of it and then you would start over again and make the changes you needed.

Find reasons to celebrate and have fun

One of the cultural norms of *moving* schools is that they celebrate; they have fun (Stoll and Fink, 1996). The staff members enjoy the pupils and each other's company. A sure sign of the attrition of change is that the exhilaration, the passion and joy of working with children and young people disappears into a 'black hole' of exhaustion, cynicism and negativity. Invitational leaders find reasons and ways to rejoice. In a world that seems to want to confess everyone else's sins, the challenge for leaders is to seize on the positive and celebrate the victories. As Linda Evans (1999) has found: 'Explicit recognition . . . leaves teachers in no doubt about how their work is rated by others. The motivational school leader conveys positive feedback in many ways, and on various occasions.'

Change also involves some losses – for example, the loss of well-practised procedures. Before moving on it is important to celebrate the past. People can go through emotions similar to the loss of a loved one when obliged to give up aspects of their approach to teaching. Paying homage to past practices and activities and the contributions of individuals to that successful past provides a necessary vehicle for moving on to a different, and in many cases a better future.

Inviting others professionally

Inviting oneself personally and professionally and inviting others personally are prerequisites to inviting others professionally (Stoll and Fink, 1996). We now turn to four ways in which leaders invite their colleagues 'professionally' to promote their learning and pupils' learning: expecting learning; organising learning; mentoring learning and monitoring learning.

. . . discover and provide the conditions under which people's learning curves go off the chart.
Barth (2001)

Expect learning

Leaders expect everyone involved in pupils' learning to strive for the highest possible standards of accomplishment. In Theodore Sizer's (1984) book, *Horace's Compromise*, a teacher agrees not to challenge certain pupils if they tacitly agree not to disrupt the class and bother him. Effective leaders hold high standards for pupil and teacher performance and, most important, for their own performance. Not only do leaders challenge practices such as Horace's that prevent learning and dehumanise pupils, high-performing leaders require pupils to adhere to reasonable standards of behaviour. Effective schools are well managed. They not only promote positive pupil behaviour; they use time wisely, and have high expectations for *all* pupils. Leaders hold themselves and their followers accountable. They enforce agreed-upon rules. They insist on teacher professionalism. Such leaders prepare their schools for inspections and if necessary, on behalf of pupils' learning, make tough decisions about using procedures to deal with rare cases of consistently underperforming teachers and support staff. Maintaining high standards of pupils' achievement, however, requires much more than mere advocacy; it involves building staff commitment and dedication through the development of a shared vision of excellence and the creation of a school culture that promotes it.

Much has been written about the importance of schools having clear goals. In Rosenholtz's (1989) learning-impoverished schools there was a lack of commitment to anything or anyone. Many reform efforts fail because participants don't have a shared sense of meaning. Bennis and Nanus (1985) argue that all organisations depend on the existence of shared meanings and interpretations of reality, which facilitate action, declaring that 'an essential factor in leadership is the capacity to influence and organize meaning for the members of the organization'. Clearly, if staff members are mutually agreed that a school's purpose is learning, then it becomes easier to come up with common goals reflecting this purpose.

Susan Drake (1995) provides a useful visual for envisioning learning across the curriculum (see Figure 5.1).

The idea of this model is that a school's community focuses up to what they want their pupils *to be*, then designs down to determine what

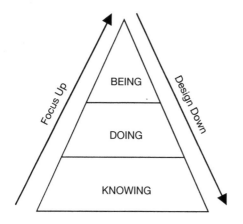

Figure 5.1 Learning across the curriculum
Source: Drake (1995)

they must *do* and what the pupils must *know* to achieve the ultimate learning goals at the *being* level. An important way in which leaders connect learning is by developing a shared sense of vision as to what the school wants the pupils *to be* when they leave the school. The key word here is 'shared': developing this vision involves the entire school community focusing up. Once a vision of what is to be achieved is determined, the school can focus down to the *doing* level. Leaders develop agreement among the staff as a whole as to what they must do across the school and across the curriculum to achieve these learning goals for pupils. For example, if the *to be* that the school community wants to achieve is tolerance of all people, then what policies, practices and procedures do all the staff members adhere to at the *doing* level to promote this value of tolerance? This doesn't, however, mean that everyone has to do exactly the same thing, as one high school principal in Ontario, Canada noted: 'I learned that you didn't have to have uniformity to be consistent. Most people think consistency is uniformity. I believe that diversity is a source of strength, well managed of course, and uniformity is not consistency. What we want is consistency; uniformity is a dead end street.'

The 'Drake' model of being, doing and knowing provides a structure for a useful process for building commitment to a set of directions within a school, or even within a larger community.

1. Create an organising group of people representing the various stakeholders involved. Invite participants to a minimum of a half-day session.
2. Organise them in mixed groups, explaining the purpose of the time together and describing the Drake model. To focus participants' thinking on learning in the twenty-first century it is useful to have a speaker or video highlighting the changing nature of society and changing understanding of learning.
3. Ask the groups to answer the question, 'What do you want young people *to be* when they leave school?' and develop a list on chart paper. After half an hour collect the sheets. During a break, the organising group develops a collective list of no more than 10 items. The group lists will look remarkably similar and include such *to be*'s as literate, numerate, tolerant, confident, able to relate to others, etc.
4. Now you have a list of *to be*'s, you need to develop some *to do*'s. Assign each group with a different *to be*, e.g. one group focuses on literacy, another on tolerance, etc. For each topic groups need to answer the question, 'What should our school and its community *do* to promote literacy, numeracy, etc.?'. Then ask each person in each group to interview three people in other groups representing different stakeholder roles. Reassemble the groups and on chart paper ask them to share their recommendations on what the school (and community) should *do* on the topic assigned. After a brief feedback session collect all the sheets.
5. The organising group takes the flipchart sheets away and synthesises them. This synthesis built around the *to be*'s should provide direction as to what the school and the community might do to achieve the purposes defined. A second session in which the synthesis is reviewed by the original participants will provide a direction document as well as building commitment and meaning to achieve important school goals.

For dedication to high standards of learning to move beyond rhetoric and good intentions it must become part of the school's culture. Culture can broadly be defined as the 'the way we do things around here' (Bolman and Deal, 1997). School culture can be seen in the signs, symbols and ceremonies in the school. It expresses itself in the way the school conducts its assemblies, defines its various roles and responsibilities, and displays learning, for example, photos of teachers learning. Failed school improvement initiatives in the past appear to have a missing ingredient: a need to reculture schools and their larger systems (Hargreaves *et al.*, 1996; Fink and Stoll, 1998). Traditional school cultures may well be inimical to the kind of learning necessary to prepare our pupils for a very different world than the one in which we grew up. In Chapter 6 we look at approaches to reculturing.

Norms are unspoken rules for what is regarded as acceptable behaviour and action within a school. Gareth Morgan (1997) explains: 'Life within a given culture flows smoothly only insofar as one's behaviour conforms with unwritten codes. Disrupt these norms and the ordered reality of life inevitably breaks down.' Norms also shape reactions to internally or externally proposed or imposed improvements. In a previous publication (Stoll and Fink, 1996), two of us identified 10 interconnected cultural norms influencing school improvement. These are reproduced below with the catchphrases that articulate the core messages of each.

1. Shared goals – 'We know where we're going'.
2. Responsibility for success – 'We can succeed'.
3. Collegiality – 'We're working on this together'.
4. Continuous improvement – 'We can get better'.
5. Lifelong learning – 'Learning is for everyone'.
6. Risk taking – 'We learn by trying something new'.
7. Support – 'There's always someone there to help'.
8. Mutual respect – 'Everyone has something to offer'.
9. Openness – 'We can discuss our differences'.
10. Celebration and humour – 'We feel good about ourselves'.

Leaders need to understand their schools' norms and work with colleagues to develop learning-friendly norms because a school's acceptance of improvement initiatives depends on the fit between the norms embedded in the changes and those within the school's own culture (Sarason, 1996).

Organise learning

Have you ever driven to work and arrived at your classroom or office and you can't remember the trip? We suspect this scenario will sound familiar. It is almost like your car is on 'cruise control', operating itself. While change is a significant part of life in schools, many things are quite predictable. There will be new pupils, staff and parents, so induction procedures should be planned and activated. Unfortunately, bullying occurs on many playgrounds; procedures should exist that all staff members enforce. Reporting to parents, governors' meetings, and many other predictable events in a school can be planned, scheduled and routinely managed. In effect, there are countless predictable procedures and practices that must be put on 'cruise control'. People must not only be able to trust the leadership; they must also be able to trust the policies, practices and established routines. James (2000) describes this as 'the engineering (operations, systems maintenance) side of leadership'. It is no accident that when new leaders 'turn around' schools experiencing difficulties they attend to the 'engineering side of leadership' (National Commission on Education, 1996; Stoll and Myers, 1998; Mortimore *et al.*, 2000). Such details are fundamental to setting the stage for learning.

The creation of policies and procedures that people trust enables the school staff to co-ordinate learning both vertically – from year level to year level – and across the school. To return to Susan Drake's model, year groups, classes, Key Stages, subjects and departments at the doing level need to be co-ordinated to ensure pupils' learning across the curriculum is consistent with the values and directions determined at the *being* level of Drake's model. At the *knowing* level, for example, how is the history or geography teacher or Key Stage 2 teacher building into their curriculum learning about the need for tolerance, or is it just assumed that this is part of a separate pastoral curriculum? Leaders are responsible for connecting the *being, doing* and *knowing* levels as well as connecting learning at each level. How does the entire staff collaborate to promote 'tolerance' or literacy or numeracy or technological literacy or positive pupil behaviour at the *doing* level? At the *knowing* level, how does the staff ensure a consistent and unified approach to problem solving across the various subjects and classrooms? A key role of leadership in schools is this ability to make these connections to build a coherent approach to pupils' learning. As one Scottish primary teacher in the Improving School Effectiveness Project responded when asked about her headteacher's leadership: 'Superb. She knows everything that goes on. She knows the curriculum, the children, the staff inside out, she picks up on your attributes. She brings out the best in everybody. She knows how her school wants to be' (Stoll *et al.*, 2001).

Many improvement initiatives are co-ordinated by groups or cadres of network leaders, whose responsibility it is to act as staff development leaders and to generate improvement through modelling and helping others change practice.

Traditionally, educational change has tended to mean only altering the use of time, space, roles and responsibilities and decision-making patterns. There is little evidence that changes in structure, *per se*, improve pupils' learning (Elmore, 1995) and classroom practice. Changing structures to 'organise learning' may well be crucial to success. Changes in the organisation of time, space, roles and responsibilities may contribute to a climate for improvement by creating new structures or eliminating inhibiting barriers to effective working relationships – for example, arranging the timetable so that teachers can work together, locating the staff room in a place that is accessible to all staff, or creating task groups from across the school to come up with creative solutions to curricular issues.

Mentor learning

One of the most powerful ways leaders can lead others' learning is through modelling. We have already described ways in which leaders can invite themselves professionally and this includes being mentored (Bolam *et al.*, 1995). Leadership also involves mentoring, and successful mentors also model learning. Barth (1990) attests to 'the extraordinary influence of modeling behavior':

> Do as I do, as well as do as I say, is a winning formula. If principals want students and teachers to take learning seriously, if they are interested in building a community of leaders, they must not only

be head teachers . . . or instructional leaders. They must above all, be *head learners*.

In addition to modelling learning, leaders need to mentor potential leaders as a means to sustain and deepen change initiatives over time and ensure effective succession planning.

> Consider the following questions adapted from Fletcher's (2000) work on teacher mentoring:
>
> What do I bring to the mentoring relationship?
> How can I communicate what I know about leadership to those I mentor?
> Am I prepared to be more than an instructor and a coach?
> Am I willing to open my own practice to the scrutiny of potential leaders?
> Am I willing to support, challenge and educate potential leaders?
> Do I understand that the dynamics and focus of my role must change?
> Am I prepared for the sacrifices, changes and challenges this will entail?

One of our mentors used to say: 'I will know when I have succeeded as a leader when I work myself out of a job.' He was a leader who led less and facilitated more. He actively supported everyone's learning, valued his own learning, recommended courses to take and schools to visit, people to talk to, appropriate reading and projects to pursue. Making teachers' learning possible means doing what is needed to provide an appropriate learning context – adequate time, sufficient space and necessary materials. It also means paying attention to teachers' emotional needs, promoting the kind of collaboration that supports adults' learning, encouraging, supporting and involving staff in meaningful school-wide decision-making, and creating learning opportunities (for example, using staff meetings for learning).

Monitor learning

Schools, like other organisations, tend to move between continuity and change, stability and chaos, creativity and consolidation, conflict and cohesion, reinforcing and limiting processes, 'clock time' and the ebb and flow of natural time. In a sense, a dialectic emerges between these paradoxical forces. A school leaning too far towards continuity and consolidation can become a 'cruising' school – a school that appears effective but does not have a capacity for change and will in time become ineffective. Conversely some schools can literally overdose on change and innovation and overreach to the point where they experience 'entropy' and in some cases death, or at least closure (Fletcher *et al.*, 1985; Riley, 1998; Fink, 2000). The challenge for leaders is to promote synthesis among paradoxical forces affecting schools through continual rethinking of purposes, and reflection on policies and practices. Review and introspection should not occur only when OFSTED knocks on the door: it should be 'extensive, internal and integral to the day-to-day life of the school' (MacBeath and Myers, 1999).

This means regular visits to classrooms to monitor learning and teaching, discussions with pupils, examining their work, and regular teacher appraisal, not only for purposes of performance management. Through effective appraisal, leaders know and can support each class's learning. One of our former leaders said, 'I do people things during the day and paper things at night'. It was not unusual to see him sitting with a group of pupils doing a science experiment, or contributing to a group discussion in English. He truly 'managed by walking around' (Peters and Waterman, 1982).

Figure 5.2 illustrates the connections between the professional and personal aspects of invitational leadership for learning.

. . . And it's about time

Steven Covey (1989) tells the story of the man who laboured mightily to saw through a tree. When an observer suggested that he might be more successful if he sharpened the saw, the worker replied that he didn't have time – he was too busy sawing the tree. Leadership roles are tremendously time-consuming. It seems everyone wants a piece of you. In inviting others professionally, a balance has to be found between going

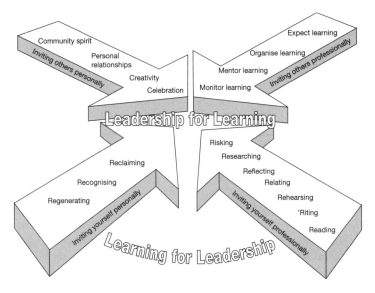

Figure 5.2 Leadership for learning: learning for leadership

too fast, which can lead to resistance, and going too slow, which can lead to stagnation. Peter Vaill (1989) describes this balance as 'the envelope of optimal realism'. Inviting others personally is critical to this

> *The value of life lies not in the length of days, but in the use you make of them.*
>
> *Montaigne*

envelope. Moreover, new learning takes time. The problem isn't the lack of time but rather our use of it. If we organise our days and weeks a little better and find time to 'sharpen the saw' then our productivity increases and our mental well-being improves. As some headteachers that one of us worked with told us, in relation to time: 'Take it. Make it.'

Time management is such an idiosyncratic thing that it is difficult to offer suggestions that have broad application. Here are a few ideas we find useful.

SAY NO SLOWLY

We can't do everything, so learn to place activities in priority and when someone asks for your involvement in a low-priority activity say, 'Thank you, I'm sure that your activity will be a great success and I appreciate your asking me but I have a personal commitment'. People will respect that.

ENRICH SUPPORT STAFF'S ROLES

Involve them, train them to perform roles that will enhance the school, build their personal efficacy, use their skills and find time for you.

SCHEDULE UNSTRUCTURED TIME

A former colleague used to schedule one hour after lunch for private reflection and asked that people respect this 'thinking time'. Cherish unstructured time and space. This is often how real learning occurs. The 'my door is always open' idea is wonderful in theory, but often impractical and inefficient in practice because some individuals can be time-wasters.

TRY 'STANDING AND WALKING MEETINGS'

Meetings are great time-eaters. If no one sits down, business is dealt with quickly. When two of us worked together, we would often 'sharpen the saw' by going for a walk together. We both refreshed ourselves and got through a tremendous amount of business.

DO A PERIODIC TIME STUDY OF YOUR OWN WORK WEEK OR MONTH

Covey (1989) suggests categorising your activities under four headings: urgent and important, not urgent but important, urgent but not important, neither urgent nor important. He suggests that the latter two categories are time-wasters and should be eliminated or delegated. You are in Covey's words 'deep in the thick of thin things'. If you spend too much time in the important and urgent category then you are managing by crisis and need to plan better by taking the time in the not urgent but important area to develop strategies to ensure that the important things are done well.

And it's about timing

Most educational books focus on change. In today's world it is the leader as change agent who gets the glory and the praise. Continuity, however, is equally important. Leadership should be regarded as a force that not only changes but also protects and intensifies a school's present idea structure in a way that enhances meaning and significance for pupils, parents and teachers, as well as members of the school's local community (Sergiovanni, 2000a). Effective leaders have or develop an exquisite sense of timing. Indeed, 'Leadership in continuously improving schools not only expands, but changes over time' (West, Jackson, Harris and Hopkins, 2000). When to push for change and when to act as a gatekeeper to protect colleagues from overload has become an increasingly important decision for leaders.

In a culture of constant change and unceasing improvement efforts, many teachers have become stressed and some even burned out. The history of innovative schools is replete with evidence of 'overreaching' and never taking the time to 'shift gears' to consolidate change through effective policies and procedures. Continuity is not only important for the emotional health of teachers but also vital for ongoing change efforts. Exhausted teachers make very poor change agents. Conversely, continuity can easily become immobility and stagnation. A leadership challenge is to maintain a school's momentum in creative and exciting ways – 'creative continuity'. Perhaps a school could streamline its parents' evenings, or develop a programme for pupils using staff and community expertise, or arrange a community picnic or a spelling contest – anything to keep people's creative juices flowing.

Based on work with and studies of a number of national and multinational businesses, Linda Gratton (2000) concludes: 'When it comes to time, there is something very special about people . . . The past, the present and the future are vital aspects of how we see the world. And the timescales for human capital are measured in years, rather than minutes, hours or months.' She provides a set of questions that highlight key aspects of time, some of which we have adapted slightly.

The relationship between the past, the present and the future

1. How strong and compelling is the learning vision for the future? How committed are individuals to this vision?
2. Are there policies and practices in place to prepare individuals for the future and which acknowledge the future for individuals?
3. How are leaders at all levels appraised? Are there reward mechanisms in place to reinforce building future competence?
4. How long do people remain in a role? Is the 'unwritten rule of the game' that the people with the highest potential stay less than two years?
5. How much emphasis is there on the aspects of the 'longer-term' cycle, particularly teacher and school development?

The time for changes in performance

1. What are the dominant time frames for setting targets and objectives, and for measuring achievement and performance? Are there measures of achievement and performance that extend further than the annual cycle?
2. Is there an understanding that implementing development initiatives will take a number of years? Are there plans in place which acknowledge this?
3. Are the core people processes relatively stable or are they frequently changed in a relatively *ad hoc* manner?
4. Do you feel that short-term tactics overwhelm longer-term considerations? If so, how can you change this?

What's in it for schools?

Invitational leadership looks at leadership in a holistic way. While this chapter has sketched a set of generic learnings, both personal and professional, applying these learnings will occur in different ways in leaders' different contexts. In each situation, the interrelations and interconnections will be unique and often unpredictable. In a world of complex and paradoxical social forces, it is this connectedness that successful leaders contribute to their schools. In a sense, as in the children's puzzle, leaders 'connect the dots' (Friedman, 2000) representing the infinite number of forces shaping a school. While many 'dots' are similar to those in other schools, many in each school are different and combine in unique ways. This is why leadership is a shifting, changing journey, with vague and changing maps. For pupils to learn, their teachers must learn, and to enable learning for both, leaders must learn how to invite themselves and others both personally and professionally.

It is insufficient for schools as organisations to promote the learning of individuals and groups. The entire organisation as a system must develop the culture and attributes of a learning organisation. It is to this topic that we turn in Chapter 6.

> Go to the people
> Live among them
> Start with what they know
> And when the deed is done
> The mission accomplished
> Of the best leaders
> The People will say
> We did it ourselves
> > Lao Tzu

Further reading

The leadership literature is voluminous, but heavily business oriented. The following books provide useful insights into educational leadership. We have picked books we feel offer something for leaders of schools in all phases.

Busher and Harris with Wise in their book *Subject Leadership and School Improvement* skilfully link the literatures on school improvement and educational leadership. With its focus on leading for teaching and learning in general and subject areas in particular, this book provides a readable and practical support for leaders at all levels in education.

Leithwood and his colleagues provide a helpful tour of the literature on educational leadership in *Changing Leadership for Changing Times*. They first detail the characteristics of types of educational leadership and then develop in considerable detail their notion of transformational leadership.

Interesting insights into variations in leadership in different countries (England, Scotland, Denmark and Australia) can be found in *Effective School Leadership*, edited by John MacBeath.

Educational Leadership and Learning, by Sue Law and Derek Glover, summarises a large body of leadership research, providing cameos along the way, as well as reflective questions and actions leaders might follow.

Sergiovanni's discussion of 'moral' leadership, while somewhat dated, is still a good read and provides a useful counterpoint to those who would reduce leadership to a management function.

Starratt's book *The Drama of Leadership* captures the idea of leadership as an art form. Both Sergiovanni and Starratt attend to the non-rational aspects of leadership and provide a useful balance to authors who see leadership as strictly a 'neck-up activity'.

Michael Fullan's latest book, *Leading in a Culture of Change*, suggests there are five core leadership competencies that apply both to educational and business leaders.

In Leading the Learning School, Colin Weatherley provides useful advice and examples to help leaders become leaders of learning. This accessible and pragmatic handbook should prove useful to both formal and informal leaders.

6 The learning community: learning together and learning from one another

Imagine two schools. In the first, pupils are learning, teachers are learning and leaders are learning. The second is a learning community. What has it got that's extra? This school knows how to put it all together, involving everyone – including parents and the community – in a collective enterprise that ensures that individual learning adds up to a coherent whole, driven by high-quality pupil learning as its fundamental purpose. Teachers' and leaders' learning don't take place for their own sake, but are absolutely essential pieces of improving learning for pupils.

In this chapter we contend that it isn't sufficient just for individuals to be learning. To succeed in a world characterised by rapid change and increased complexity, it is vital that schools can grow, develop, adapt creatively to change and take charge of change so that they can create their own preferable future. Ability to take charge of externally driven change, rather than being controlled by it, has been shown to distinguish schools that are more effective and more rapidly improving from ones that are not (Rosenholtz, 1989; Hopkins et al., 1994; Stoll and Fink, 1996; Gray et al., 1999). More than 20 years ago, Chris Argyris and Donald Schön maintained that an organisation's key challenge isn't to become more effective at performing a stable task in the light of stable purposes, but to 'restructure its purposes and redefine its task in the face of a changing environment' (1978). This is even truer today when it regularly feels like we are trying to build castles on shifting sand.

In the words of Per Dalin: 'The only way schools will survive the future is to become creative learning organizations. The best way students can learn how to live in the future is to experience the life of the "learning school"' Dalin with Rolff (1993). Such a challenge requires more than pupils, teachers and leaders learning. It depends on collective commitment of the entire school community. Learning communities know how to deal with and creatively take charge of change because they have a collective understanding of where they are going and what is important. They are open to new ideas and create new ways of learning and working to deal with complex situations. Their cultures are learning-friendly, promoting and supporting new learning practices and creating new knowledge and understanding.

We start the chapter by looking at learning communities and suggesting that they have a lot in common with learning organisations, but that community is especially important in schools. The learning community not only involves the school's staff as learners but also actively engages its parents, pupils and the wider community in learning that enhances the organisation's purposes. We then consider the influences on learning communities and what enhances and inhibits their learning. Finally, as in other chapters, we examine the time implications and ask 'What's in it for schools?'

What do we know about being a learning community?

Coral Mitchell and Larry Sackney (2000) define a learning community as 'a group of people who take an active, reflective, collaborative, learning-oriented, and growth-promoting approach toward the mysteries, problems and perplexities of teaching and learning'. To us, being a learning community is also a state of mind, is not linear, is bigger than the sum of its parts, and is about learning as a community.

It's a state of mind

Schools that are learning communities have a mindset that helps people understand how they can influence their own destiny and create knowledge they can use. In common with the learning organisation, members of the learning community understand that they create their own reality and can, therefore, shape it. Peter Senge has described a learning organisation as one that is 'continually expanding its capacity to create its future' (Senge, 1990). Senge believes any organisation truly engaged in organisational learning has experienced 'metanoia' – a shift in mind.

It's not linear

Organisational learning doesn't mean 'if we do X then Y will happen'. Those people who have been a teacher or leader in more than one school, who have found that something that worked in the first school doesn't work in the next school, will understand this all too well. This is because the processes and effects of learning influence each other in a reciprocal way. In other words, the consequences of people's actions influence what happens next, and every influence can be both a cause and an effect. This concept of feedback challenges the notion that organisational learning can be achieved by linear or mechanistic means (Reed and Stoll, 2000). What it requires instead is 'thinking in circles' (O'Connor and McDermott, 1997).

For example, a school with attendance problems in Year 8 tries a procedure of rewards and sanctions. Attendance problems increase. The school then needs to investigate the rewards and sanctions procedure to see why it hasn't had a positive influence. Through further enquiry, it finds that pupils' parents are unaware their children are missing school. The head of year then phones the home of every pupil who hasn't arrived by 10 a.m., and this increases attendance. The school then reflects on this procedure to understand its positive influence and other side effects and benefits.

It's bigger than the sum of the parts

All of the individual learning in the world doesn't add up to collective learning. As a result of prior experiences and unique differences, learners bring with them different models of how the world operates. They have their own vision of the purpose of schools, how to go about their work and what it is important to achieve. Sometimes, as Roland Barth (1990) says, these visions are submerged and fragmentary because, in the hustle and bustle of busy school life, they haven't been examined for a long time. While learning is social, many teachers spend their work time behind closed classroom doors. David Hargreaves (1999), however, cautions that 'No single teacher knows, or could

> *There are many cases in which organisations know less than their members. There are even cases in which the organisations cannot seem to learn what every member knows.*
>
> Argyris and Schön (1978)

know, the totality of the staff's professional knowledge'. If the staff doesn't have a collective understanding of what is and should be happening in their school, what confused and conflicting messages do pupils receive? Coming to a collective, although inevitably evolving, understanding of where the school is going is a central feature of a real learning community.

It's about learning as community

Linking the words 'learning' and 'community' can produce several possibilities for schools: learning *of* community; learning *from* community; learning *with* community; learning *for* community; and learning *as* community.

LEARNING OF COMMUNITY

If those in schools want to see their preferred futures come true, they need the support of their community. It is therefore critical for them to educate the community; to help them understand what they are doing, why and how the community can best support them because: 'Within the classroom setting there are in fact three actors ever present – the teacher, the student, and the parent(s), who are 'present' in the sense that the beliefs, attitudes, and habits of mind of the family are thoroughly embedded in the mind of the child' (Coleman, 1998).

We have come across many opportunities for the community outside schools to learn in schools. Members of the community can engage in practical sessions on aspects of the curriculum or how to help their children read, ICT training, and English-language lessons. Highlighting the importance of the home environment to pupils' achievement, one recent Australian study (Silins and Mulford, 2002) concludes that schools need to work with parents to help them understand how they can best help their children and provide a supportive home environment.

LEARNING FROM COMMUNITY

Some schools involve parents and other members of the community in sharing a particular area of expertise, whether it is extra-curricular pottery or offering financial advice as a governor. Companies are increasingly encouraging employees to have this kind of experience, not simply as a form of community service but as an integral part of continuing professional development and 'peoplistic' skills.

LEARNING WITH COMMUNITY

As well as parental volunteers going with their children and teachers to learn together on educational visits, some schools provide opportunities for families to learn together. With an ageing population, the potential for grandparents, and even great grandparents, to help with children's learning is enormous. This works both ways. Young people can help with their grandparents' learning, and families and extended families can engage in intergenerational collaborative learning. Involving parents as more equal partners in a two-way dialogue about learning and teaching is still relatively rare, as one of us found in a study of teachers involved in school reform efforts (Hargreaves *et al.*, 2001).

> Involving parents in (and not just informing them about) common learning standards or outcomes creates opportunities to develop a deeper dialogue between parents and teachers about teaching and learning . . .
>
> Hargreaves *et al.* (2001)

LEARNING FOR COMMUNITY

One of UNESCO's four fundamental pillars is *learning to live together*. Here the purpose of learning is to promote citizenship and positive relationships. One example is older pupils helping their younger peers, for example the Year 7 pupils in one school we know working with their teacher to develop geography materials for Year 6 pupils in one of their feeder schools. Another example is service learning, through involvement with groups such as Community Service Volunteers. Citizenship education is firmly established on the national agenda, promoting social and moral responsibility, community involvement and political literacy.

LEARNING AS COMMUNITY

In a learning community, everything people do on a daily basis, within the school and in relation to parents and the local community, is underpinned by a sense of belonging and collective commitment to each other's learning and ensuring that the school is *moving*. Tom Sergiovanni (2000b) argues that to become a true learning community a school must also be a: community of relationships; community of place; community of mind and heart; community of memory; and a community of practice.

What influences collective learning?

A school is a social learning context. This provides a backdrop for the learning that takes place and influences the nature of that learning. In short, if the context isn't favourable, collective learning will be inhibited, but if the influences are favourable, learning will be enhanced. There are a number of influences within this social learning context (Stoll, 1999 – see Figure 6.1).

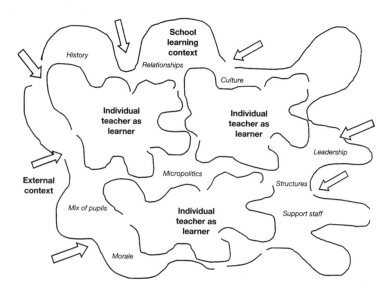

Figure 6.1 School influences on collective learning

Source: Based on Stoll (1999)

RELATIONSHIPS

Working together productively in schools depends on positive relationships. Successful schools share many attributes of caring families, but in some schools, just like in some families, relationships are dysfunctional. Healthy relationships provide a secure basis for learning.

CULTURE

Michael Fullan (1992) has argued that any attempt to improve a school not addressing school culture is 'doomed to tinkering' because school culture influences readiness for change. Indeed, it can either be a black hole or a fertile garden for improvement (Stoll, 1999). The heart of school culture is the deeper level of basic beliefs and values shared by those in the school. These create a mindset for the school about itself and its environment. Each school has a different reality of school life and how to go about its work. Previously, two of us described five cultures of schools: moving, cruising, strolling, struggling and sinking (Stoll and Fink, 1996 – see Figure 6.2). Attempting collective learning is a very different matter in a cruising school than in a moving school.

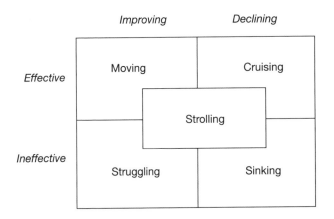

Figure 6.2 Five school cultures
Source: Stoll and Fink (1996)

POWER ISSUES

Schools are full of internal politics (Ball, 1987): they are places in which control is a key issue. Some teachers want to influence school decisions; others want to be left alone. Sarason (1990) maintains that educational reforms continuously fail because attention isn't paid to altering power relationships. In some schools, however, positive politics are promoted (Blase, 1998), such that people's natural political activities within school contribute to the school's goals.

STRUCTURES

Schools are bounded by structures shaping their capacity to learn and respond to change. Traditional egg-carton compartmentalised school designs inhibit collaboration, whereas more flexible architectural designs are more likely to support collaborative cultures. The size of the school and classes within it, the physical buildings, location of the staff room and how the school day is divided are all examples of structures. Structures can inhibit capacity or support its growth.

LEADERSHIP

We argued the importance of leadership in the previous chapter. Collective learning is dependent on leadership for and of learning.

MORALE

Some schools are better places to be than others. In response to a survey item in the Improving School Effectiveness Project, large differences between schools were found in the number of teachers reporting that they liked working there. In two schools in similarly deprived areas (Stoll *et al.*, 2001), every teacher in one school responded positively to this item, while fewer than a fifth of teachers in the other school did so, and almost a third felt the school had got worse 'as a place to be' over the previous two years.

HISTORY

Like other organisations, schools go through lifecycles. During some periods they are 'ripe for improvement'. At other times, often depending on the staff at the time, the leadership, and whether previous efforts at innovation have been successful or otherwise, there may be institutional 'inertia'. A school, where one of us taught when it was new and innovative and then studied retrospectively, looking back over 25 years, went through years of creativity and experimentation followed by years of 'overreaching' and entropy. Finally it settled into survival and continuity, no different from many surrounding schools (Fink, 2000). Per Dalin (1993) charts the stages in schools' lifecycles (see Table 6.1).

What stage are you at in your school's life cycle? What would it take for you to move to the next stage (see Table 6.1)?

MIX OF PUPILS

The pupils attending a school flavour it in a particular way through their own pupil culture and peer-group processes of how they relate and act as a group (Thrupp, 1999). This is influenced by their age, as well as the mix of girls and boys, pupils from different social class, ethnic and cultural backgrounds, and those with special learning needs.

Table 6.1 Schools' life cycles

Fragmented school	No common understanding of its needs. Change initiatives don't result from joint staff discussions. Changes need a lot of external support.
Project school	Innovative drive comes from management and the school leader. A history of innovation, however, does exist, and there is ongoing development of common goals.
Organic school	Resembles a learning organisation. It's open for internal and external change initiatives, knows its own strengths and weaknesses, and can cope with and learn from improvement processes. This school creates its own innovation history and experience.

Source: Based on Dalin with Rolff (1993)

SUPPORT STAFF

These staff play a significant role in the lives of a school. Many live in the local area and are connected to the local community. The extent of their involvement and interest in the school as a whole, and the ways in which they facilitate learning, are all potential influences on collective learning.

> ... *improving and exemplary schools*
> ... *are characterised by a passion*
> *for learning* ...
>
> *Hopkins (2001a)*

How might these influences inhibit collective learning?

Collective learning isn't easy. Several things can get in the way. Building a learning community depends on understanding the influences on it and the role you may be playing in their existence. So, for example, every teacher, headteacher, support teacher, pupil, parent and governor has an image in their mind of what their school should be, how it should run, what learning means, and so on. Put these together and you can get a real 'hotchpotch' of mental maps and plenty of room for conflict. Peter Senge (1990) explains that 'new insights fail to get put into practice because they conflict with deeply held internal images of how the world works, images that limit us to familiar ways of thinking and acting'.

Similarly, poor communication, dysfunctional relationships or power struggles between any of the following need to be addressed so that they don't inhibit collective learning: staff; leaders and other staff; staff and pupils; pupils; the school and governors; and the school and its community. Low morale is another collective-learning crusher, highlighted by signs that people don't enjoy working in the school, lack of trust and openness, and few opportunities to celebrate. Another problem is stress and work intensification, where people appear to be overworked, exhausted and showing signs of burnout. External pressures can also inhibit collective learning. We discuss these in the final chapter.

One inhibitor we have encountered is the cruising-school mentality (Stoll and Fink, 1998). Cruising schools have powerful norms that challenge collective learning. These norms are conserved through socialisation and control systems (Levitt and March, 1988), creating an organisational memory of unspoken rules and procedures to follow. If your school's memory tells you it's not a good idea to try out a new learning approach because new ideas take a lot of effort and are often not successful, it's hard to change this mentality.

Cruising-school norms include:

1. Contentment – 'If it ain't broke, don't fix it'.
2. Avoidance of commitment – 'Let's send it to a committee'.
3. Goal diffusion – 'We do our own thing but we do it well'.
4. Reactive – 'Let's wait and see'.
5. Perpetuating total top-down leadership – 'It's your job, not mine'.
6. Conformity – 'Don't rock the boat'.
7. Nostalgia – 'Things used to be great around here'.
8. Blaming others – '"They" are pushing new ideas down our throats'.
9. Congeniality – 'We all get along'.
10. Denial – 'The research and data are biased'.

Learning communities attend to potential blocks to collective learning by understanding and working on negative influences such as these.

> Rate each of the cruising-school norms on the following five-point scale: 5 = not at all true in my school; 4 = occasionally true in my school; 3 = sometimes true in my school; 2 = fairly widespread in my school; 1 = a pretty accurate description of my school.
>
> Working with the norms that you have rated 1, 2 or 3, what steps can you take to change them?
>
> For each of the norms rated 4 or 5, how can you ensure that they do not become an issue in your school?

What processes enhance learning for community?

How, then, does a school harness individual acts of learning of pupils, teachers and leaders to create a learning community? Six processes positively influence the organisational learning of schools (see Figure 6.3). In a school actively learning, these processes occur concurrently as the school goes about its daily business, although some may be more important than others at different times.

Figure 6.3 Learning community processes

Community dialogue

Garmston and Wellman (1995) point out that: 'Continuous renewal in complex human systems requires ongoing dialogue within the organization and between the organization and its environment'. Arriving at a shared sense of meaning about where you are going as a school and working to adapt your goals in the light of messages from your context are critical features of a learning community. How does truly shared meaning evolve into a vision about the future? Developing shared purpose is an ongoing process of dialogue between leaders, teachers, support staff, pupils, parents, governors, the local community, other schools, LEAs, businesses, colleges and universities, policy makers, unions and others with a stake in schools. It ultimately builds a community of learners, involving them deeply and democratically, and constantly reaching out and working beyond the school. This is more than parents' evenings and sending home newsletters; more than inviting local businesses to an open day. It's not a one-off: it's ongoing, and means communicating in a fundamentally different way so that collective new learning insights can blossom.

In schools, as in many organisations, a lot of discussion takes place. David Bohm (1985), a physicist who wrote about dialogue, didn't view discussion as serious because it avoids 'undiscussables', lying below the surface and blocking true and honest communication. People also bring deeply held assump-

> . . . 'dialogue', the capacity of members of a team to suspend assumptions and enter into a genuine 'thinking together'. . . allowing the group to discover insights not attainable individually.
>
> Senge (1990)

tions to discussion, defending them hotly when challenged. Dialogue is a more open process, going beyond any individual's understanding, encouraging people 'to participate in a pool of shared meaning that leads to aligned action' (Jaworski, 1998), although it doesn't necessarily require people to agree with each other. We found, when writing this book, that we brought with us different assumptions about certain topics. Discussion and debate didn't get us very far. The common understandings enabling us to move our thinking on and come up with a book that represents all three of us collectively have come through dialogue.

Bohm believed three basic conditions are necessary for dialogue:

1. All participants *suspending their assumptions*, making them open to questioning and observation.
2. All participants *regarding one another as colleagues* – as Peter Senge (1990) explains: 'Thinking of each other as colleagues is important because thought is participative. The conscious act of thinking of each other as colleagues contributes toward interacting as colleagues. This may sound simple, but it can make a profound difference.'
3. Having a *facilitator who 'holds the context'* of the dialogue – without a skilled facilitator, natural thought habits draw people back into discussion, especially early on in the process.

We have participated in and heard of dialogue in LEAs as well as schools. For example, a new unitary LEA a few years ago involved a wide range of stakeholders in a process to generate its vision. An evaluation for the LEA of its progress by one of us demonstrated high levels of satisfaction among the majority of stakeholders interviewed or responding to questionnaires. By drawing in the whole community, schools and LEAs are able to scan their context more effectively.

> How often do you engage in genuine dialogue in your school(s)? Think of some examples. What influences in your school(s) support the process of community dialogue? What influences work against the process? How can you reduce the negative influences and increase the positive influences?

Self-evaluation

Self-evaluation isn't just about data collection. It involves strategic thinking, planning and action to create useful new knowledge for the school community.

> It is an index of the nation's health when its school communities have a high level of intelligence and know how to use the tools of self-evaluation and self-improvement. . . . To know and understand learning requires the studied long-term insights and analysis of teachers and pupils reflecting together, using tools and finding the language to get inside the learning process.
>
> MacBeath (1999)

These days there is a tremendous amount of data in schools, but the approaches schools take to data are very different: some barely penetrate the surface, while others ask very serious and complex questions. Although data and statistics may provide the tools for measuring important educational concepts, the numbers are only as good as the thinking that goes into the interpretation (Earl and Katz, 2002). As Popham (1999) says, using test scores to represent quality is like 'measuring temperature with a tablespoon'. To put it another way: 'The intelligent school is comfortable and skilled in its ability to interpret and use information and put it to the service of its pupils and the organisation as a whole. The school knows how to learn from the data and what the data means' (MacGilchrist, Myers and Reed, 1997).

We have found it helpful to use inquiry-oriented questions when working with schools:

- What do you think these results tell you? Why?
- Now step outside the obvious interpretations and challenge your existing thinking and experience. What else might these results mean?
- Who are the different audiences who might be interested in these results? What questions will they want answered? What evidence will they accept that your interpretations are correct?
- What don't these results tell you? What's missing? What else do you need to know? How can you find this out? Who can help you?
- What questions do these results raise for you? How will you go about answering these questions?
- How can you use these results to help you increase your learning?

Asking the 'right' questions isn't easy. Indeed, there may be no such thing as 'the right questions'. What matters is a constant and pervasive enquiry-minded approach to work. It takes time and effort: sometimes schools need to work at this for

> *Data do not provide right answers or quick fixes. Instead, they are necessary but not sufficient elements of the conversations that ensue.*
> *Earl and Katz (2002)*

years. One of us evaluated the Manitoba School Improvement Program (MSIP) (Earl and Lee, 2000). One of the most interesting activities we observed was the change in staff attitudes and actions related to what we called 'enquiry-mindedness'. Over the years, many of them became quite adept not only at collecting data but, much more importantly, at thinking about it, interpreting it in context and using it wisely, so they were no longer in awe of data, nor were they looking for data to confirm their prejudices or endorse their practices. Instead, they were actively searching for understanding, struggling to describe the complexity of their work and using systematic inquiry procedures to stand back and think about their school.

Schools have a wealth of knowledge they can draw on. For example:

- knowledge of pupils' progress and development, learning orientation and interests
- teachers' and leaders' knowledge about their own practice
- knowledge created when teachers and leaders examine their practice systematically through action research

- knowledge from others, for example parents, governors, advisors, inspectors, community members.

But Karen Seashore Louis (1998) explains that 'schools cannot learn until there is explicit or implicit agreement about what they know – about their students, teaching and learning, and about how to change'. What distinguishes organisational learning from individual learning, Louis (1994) contends, is an additional step of collective knowledge creation. As members of the school community interact, engage in serious dialogue and deliberate about all the information they have and the data they collect, they interpret it communally and distribute it among themselves. School development plans that are living documents and involve all the school's important stakeholders are as relevant today as when they first became popular in the 1980s. It is this inclusive, evidence-based, inquiry-oriented process of creating a school development plan that is as important as, if not more important than, the actual product.

As schools are increasingly expected to use evidence (not only their own, but from elsewhere) to inform their practice, it is important to evaluate the quality of evidence and use it wisely in making decisions.

Schools can engage in three interconnected modes of inquiry (Stoll *et al.*, 2002), all of which can be done independently or in collaboration with external researchers or consultants:

1 research and evaluation across the school, in departments and by individual classroom teachers
2 a more systematic approach to collecting, analysing and using data and evidence in the course of ongoing work, for example, in relation to pupils' exam or test results, value-added data, attitude surveys, and external school inspection reports
3 seeking out and using relevant and practical research, generated by external researchers.

In relation to the third mode, research by Brad Cousins and Ken Leithwood (1993) suggests that the criteria Canadian teachers used to evaluate whether external knowledge would be used included:

- *sophistication* – quality of the information source, including appropriateness and rigour

- *credibility* – believability of the information, and expertise of those disseminating it
- *relevance* – whether the knowledge was considered useful and practical
- *communication quality* – clarity, style and readability
- *content* – whether the content confirmed or conflicted with existing knowledge, and whether it was valued, positive, and covered a topic in sufficient depth and breadth
- *timeliness* – if it was disseminated at an appropriate time and delivered in an ongoing manner.

Schools also need to remember that to prepare pupils for their future: 'the dissemination of existing good practice is an inadequate basis for making a success of schools . . . to be content with current knowledge and practice is to be left behind' (Hargreaves, 1999). To this end, David Hargreaves suggests teachers in knowledge-creating schools use to their advantage 'a ubiquitous feature of classrooms' – 'tinkering' with practice, elaborating on it and extending it to support collective knowledge creation. As they share and develop these ideas, team learning is enhanced.

Team learning

In Chapters 4 and 5 we looked at learning for which teachers and leaders take responsibility. Here we argue that a key process in the development of a learning community is ensuring that these are not individual or isolated learning experiences but ongoing, collective professional learning where teachers learn from and in practice (Ball and Cohen, 1999) in communities of practice (Wenger, 1998). Opportunities for teachers and leaders to learn, process and understand their learning experiences together are essential. This is when the kind of shared meaning we have described often evolves. A single focused question at a staff meeting can open up a whole learning dialogue. For example, 'What do people mean when they talk about assessment *for* learning?' Opportunities for teachers to work and learn together are part of 'an optimal school learning environment' (Smylie, 1995).

Learning is a social process, as we have explained. Learning teams may come together, for example, to explore how thinking skills can better be incorporated across their school's curriculum. They might arrange rotational observations in each other's classrooms, choosing a particular thinking-skills focus, and then arrange a joint debrief where they explore not only the experience in that particular class but also cross-curricular implications. Peter Cuttance and colleagues (in Cuttance 2001) found that just about the most important outcome of the Australian 107-school Innovations and Best Practice Project was its lessons for teacher learning:

> The most powerful innovations incorporated teams of teachers learning by 'working' with new knowledge and, in the process, enhancing their understanding of the learning needs and capacities of their students. In these 'learning teams', teachers played a variety of roles. Models of professional development based on the dissemination of information are inadequate for supporting teachers in their role in the emerging knowledge society. Professional learning requires active engagement and work on the knowledge being developed by teachers.
>
> Stokes and Cuttance (2001)

When two of us were involved in the Effective Schools Project in the Halton Board of Education, Ontario (Stoll and Fink, 1996), the most effective professional development always involved components on assessing, understanding and dealing with change over time, conflict resolution, the influence of school culture, leadership and team building. This was irrespective of whether the specific topic was assessment for learning, co-operative group learning, improving technology across the curriculum or school development planning. As we have argued, learning means change and learning is social. Indeed, the social time together is as important as the learning content, and high-quality professional development builds this in. Real school-wide change requires people to learn together. In the experience of Little, 'we uncovered the most supportive learning environments for students in those schools – or more often, in pockets within schools – where teacher development was also valued and supported' (Little, 2001).

INSET can be seen as 'planned event, series of events or extended programme of accredited or non-accredited learning' (Day, 1999). While it is not the all-encompassing answer to teachers' learning needs, Chris Day found, in a small study, that successful INSET met six specific needs:

- *targeting needs* – relevant, focusing on needs specific to the age range taught
- *content needs* – reinforcing existing thinking, while increasing knowledge and awareness, and encouraging different ways of examining issues
- *utilisation needs* – directly applicable to practice and enhanced curriculum development
- *process needs* – offering a balance of well-structured activities, enabling participants to work with colleagues and share experiences
- *leadership/modelling needs* – well-prepared, enthusiastic, caring tutors, who understood group dynamics
- *time and energy needs* – time away from their busy classrooms allowed teachers the space to reflect.

Bruce King and Fred Newmann (2001) are studying nine urban elementary schools across the USA with school-wide professional learning communities. They conclude that professional development is only effective in boosting teaching and learning quality if it focuses on professional community among the whole staff, as well as knowledge, skills and dispositions of individual teachers and coherent programmes for pupil and teacher learning related to clear school goals.

Other American researchers who have studied professional community (Louis, Kruse and Associates, 1995) highlight features that are all geared towards team, rather than individual, learning:

- a common set of activities providing many occasions for face-to-face interactions, and potential for common understandings, values and expectations for behaviour to evolve
- particular organisational structures promoting this, such as time and expectations that people will gather and talk, small, stable networks of teachers, etc.
- a core of shared values about what pupils should learn, about how staff and pupils should behave, and about the shared aims to maintain and promote the community.

Tom Guskey (2000) suggests that there are five critical levels to consider when evaluating professional development: participants' reactions; participants' learning; organisational support and change;

participants' use of new knowledge and skills; and, ultimately, learning outcomes. We would add another, linked to organisational support and change – team learning.

> How do you evaluate professional development in your school(s)?

Reculturing

As new knowledge is created inevitably it is matched against the school's norms – unspoken rules – that guide what is customary or acceptable behaviour and action in the school. We have already discussed culture. An effective learning culture is not afraid to admit that 'Learning comes from joint acknowledgement of inadequacy and ignorance . . . and also possesses some confidence in its ability to grow to understanding and expertise, so that perplexity is transformed into mastery' (Claxton, 1999).

Reculturing is about visiting and challenging cultural norms, making sure they are supportive of learning. One definition of culture is proposed by Morgan: 'How organisations work when no-one is looking' (Morgan, 1997). Understanding how existing mental maps influence school norms and cultivating learning-oriented norms is essential because if the norms connected with the changes come into conflict with the school's existing norms, people in the school will find it out to accept the changes.

In Chapter 5 we described 10 norms underpinning the work of improving schools. Schools with these norms have worked hard to clarify a shared vision of what they want the school to stand for. They are facilitated by leaders who: focus on building trust, confidence and self-efficacy; emphasise high expectations; promote discussion about values related to learning and teaching; offer a range of opportunities for professional development; and adapt structures to enable teachers to work together. Two norms merit further comment in relation to their power for collective learning. The first is *collegiality*, because it creates greater interdependence, collective commitment, shared responsibility, and, perhaps most important, 'greater readiness to participate in the difficult business of review and critiques' (Fullan and Hargreaves, 1992). The second, *risk taking*, is particularly important because learning is risk taking. Experimenting, trial and error and learning through failure are essential parts of growing. They also symbolise a willingness to try something different, to consider new approaches, and to move into uncharted territory. Other norms set a climate and provide the psychological safety net that can enable risk taking to occur without danger.

Nurturing all 10 norms is a prerequisite for promoting organisational learning, although some have more specifically to say about learning than others. When, however, prevailing cultural norms inhibit learning, as in the case of cruising schools, 'unlearning' may be required to 'reprogramme' the school's memory so that norms support organisational learning. This may mean confronting people over their use of language and their assumptions, as well as finding forums in which people can openly examine their values and underlying assumptions more closely.

> 'As if community were not ambitious enough, a community of learners is ever so much more. Such a school is a community whose defining, underlying culture is one of learning. The condition for membership in the community is that one learn, continue to learn and support the learning of others. Everyone'
>
> (Barth, 2001).

Creativity and spontaneity

In a learning community, boundaries are pushed as people collectively identify new problems and transfer previous learning in new ways to solve these problems progressively over time (Seltzer and Bentley, 1999). David Perkins (1995) describes this creative process as 'learning your way around'. Inevitably, this requires being open to new ideas, open to people who think outside the box, open to the 'mavericks' on staff, open to divergent thinkers, able to live with uncertainty, willingness to take risks and make mistakes, but also having the confidence to keep going. As Mihaly Csikszentmihalyi (1996) explains, 'If you learn to be creative in everyday life . . . you will change the way you experience [the world]. Problem finding is important in the daily domain because it helps us focus on issues that will affect our experiences but otherwise may go unnoticed'.

Creativity is a state of mind in which all of our intelligences are working together. It involves seeing, thinking and innovating.

Lucas (2001)

Doing what you've always done will get you what you always got and this is inadequate for a rapidly changing world. Imagination has to be able to flourish, creating new responses, ideas and insights (O'Sullivan and West-Burnham, 1998). New ideas and innovatory thinking will be the life blood of learning communities.

Carousel brainstorming is a process we have used many times to generate ideas and solve problems. For example, you may have identified from your self-evaluation six issues that are getting in the way of pupil learning, e.g. not being able to get parents into school, pupil bullying in the playground, lack of teacher time for team learning, etc.

1. Pose each issue as a 'How do we resolve this?' kind of question on chart paper, distributed around the staff room.
2. Divide the people involved randomly into six groups (if you have too many people, have two or more sheets for each issue and create more groups).
3. Give groups a few minutes to brainstorm their first issue before moving them to the next sheet which they will read and then add ideas.
4. Repeat this process, allowing a little more time for later issues as more ideas accumulate.
5. Once this has been completed, the whole group can be involved in evaluating the issues and deciding plans of action.

Several schools have found it helpful to leave the sheets up for a few days.

Connecting everything you know

This is 'the big picture', also described as systems thinking or 'joined-up thinking'. It's about looking at the whole and seeing the relationships and patterns between the parts. It is essential to understand how the school as a whole (the system) and its constituent parts (the sub-systems) are relating to each other.

Peter Senge (1990) describes systems thinking as 'a discipline for seeing wholes'. It is a framework for seeing interrelationships rather than linear cause–effect chains, and for seeing patterns and processes of change rather than static 'snapshots'. In Senge's view, systems thinking exists when those in organisations understand how their actions shape their reality, as well as the reverse: that's the feedback part.

The capacity to see patterns and discern connections between seemingly unconnected events is a key feature of organisational learning. It's a crucial tool for improvement efforts, a basis for taking charge of change and feeling control. Systems thinking enables a school to analyse more deeply the factors that underlie its concerns and difficulties (especially where linear deductions of causality fail to get at the root issues), helping make connections within the school as a whole, its inner workings and its relation to its environment. That is why studies of schools improving pupils' learning highlight the need to attend to school-level conditions as well as necessary changes of learning and teaching (van Velzen *et al.*, 1985; Hopkins *et al.*, 1994; Stoll and Fink, 1996).

Some people say 'we have a school development plan to make sure we cover everything and achieve our priorities'. But many school development plans are not about connectedness: they don't get below the surface of the actions or explore what happens when all of the priorities are being worked on at one time. There are several frameworks, however, that can help people to look at their work and workplace in different ways to get a fuller picture, like trying various pairs of lenses and viewing the world differently with each.

Connectedness underlies Barbara MacGilchrist, Kate Myers and Jane Reed's (1997) 'intelligent school'. They argue that it's important to consider 'the wholeness of the enterprise in which schools are engaged'. Their nine intelligences for successful schools can be used by schools 'in the process of addressing simultaneously the core business of learning, teaching, effectiveness and improvement':

1 Contextual intelligence
2 Strategic intelligence
3 Academic intelligence
4 Reflective intelligence
5 Pedagogical intelligence
6 Collegial intelligence
7 Emotional intelligence
8 Spiritual intelligence
9 Ethical intelligence.

Another person who makes connections is Gareth Morgan (1997). He argues that all organisation and management theories are based on implicit images or metaphors leading us to see, understand and manage organisations in distinctive but only partial ways. Morgan believes that successful organisations have a deep understanding of situations that face them because they:

> develop the knack of reading situations with various scenarios in mind . . . have a capacity to remain open and flexible, suspending immediate judgements whenever possible, until a more comprehensive view of the situation emerges. They are aware that new insights often arise as one approaches situations from 'new angles' and that a wide and varied reading can create a wide and varied range of action possibilities. Less effective . . . problem solvers, however, seem to interpret everything from a fixed standpoint. As a result, they frequently hit blocks they cannot get around; their actions and behaviors are often rigid and inflexible.

Morgan offers eight metaphors or images of organisations: machines, organisms, brains, cultures, political systems, psychic prisons, flux and transformation, instruments of domination. He suggests that collectively they demonstrate how metaphor can be used 'to generate a range of complementary and competing insights and learn to build on the strengths of different points of view'.

Change frames

One of us has been involved in the Change Frames project, where seven frames have been identified that, taken together, help learning communities open up issues and develop strategies based on multiple perspectives as opposed to defining issues in narrow, simplistic and task-oriented ways (Hargreaves *et al.*, 2000). Implementation and, more important, sustainability of change require attention to each of the frames. Briefly, the nature and significance of each of the seven frames are as follows:

- The *purpose* frame is concerned with the moral purposes of change.
- The *emotional* frame is concerned with the feelings and emotions of educational change.

- The *political* frame is concerned with changes of power, as well as with how you create the power to bring about change.
- The *cultural* frame is concerned with the human relationships and patterned ways of acting and believing in a community that are affected by change efforts.
- The *structural* frame is concerned with how role definitions and organisations of time and space affect and are affected by educational change.
- The *organisational and professional learning* frame is concerned with how teachers and others learn to manage the particular changes being implemented as well as about how to cope with and initiate change in positive ways on an ongoing basis.
- The *leadership* frame is concerned with both the formal and informal leaders who must foster organisational coherence and also develop and preserve the kind of relationships within a school which promote organisational learning.

Consider your school development plan (for those in LEAs, consider your education development plan). How can change frames help you get the most out of the development planning process?

Take a particular problem you are currently facing. Look at it through the change frames. What have you learnt from this?

Look at a recent letter sent out to parents or your school handbook. Analyse it through the different change frames. What does it tell you about the school?

. . . And what about time?

Arriving at collective meaning and commitment is not an overnight process, much as we might want it to be. Time is perhaps the most precious resource in schools. It needs to be understood and embedded into school planning and learning. Time to meet and talk is an essential resource for a learning community (Louis, Kruse and Associates, 1995).

Norms, values and beliefs about time differ across schools. Peterson (1999) proposes a set of concepts related to time to consider when examining your school's culture:

- *Amount of time*: How much time is a lot of time? In some schools, two days of INSET is considered too much, while in others this is seen as a bare minimum for learning new ideas.
- *Time as an investment*: Is professional learning viewed as a waste of time or an important investment in pupils?
- *Rate or speed of change over time* (Schein, 1992): How fast should new ideas and techniques be incorporated into the school? Should the school focus on one reform approach (i.e. approach to school improvement) during the next three or four years, or try to adopt two or more approaches at once?
- *Time on/time off*: When can staff members relax, disengage, or rest? In some school cultures, professional development sessions are time for a respite or breather, a time to doze – perhaps not physically, but psychologically. In others, staff development time is a period of heightened attention, energy and focus.
- *Sequence of events over time* (Schein, 1992): What should be done first, second, or never? In some schools, everything but professional learning occurs first. Workshops, study groups, discussions of practice, etc. take last place to other activities.
- *Ownership of time*: Whose time is this? In some schools, the culture decrees that time is the sole property of individual teachers. In others, time is understood as shared for the good of the whole organisation.

Time spent in building a learning community will ultimately save the time wasted in acrimonious debate, false starts and frustration over aborted initiatives.

What's in it for schools?

What are the outcomes of being a learning community? Are your preferred futures likely to be achieved? What's really in it for schools? We can think of at least ten.

ENHANCED CAPACITY

You can shape your own future, to anticipate and deal with problems, create the results you want to create as well as doing the things you have to do, and improve continuously.

ADAPTIVITY

You are able to change what you do while staying true to your core purpose because you have confidence about who you are and where you're going.

RECULTURED

Where necessary, you will have challenged and changed inappropriate norms, replacing them with norms that value and support learning.

WIDER CHOICE OF POSSIBLE BEHAVIOURS

You will have a broader repertoire of how to deal with different situations; you aren't defensive or afraid to try something different.

RESTRUCTURED

Where necessary you will have amended structures, replacing them with flexible structures (policies, etc.) that can be changed again as the need arises.

NEW KNOWLEDGE CREATED

You have organisational knowledge about your mental maps and how you work best.

REAL TEAM LEARNING

You have collective commitment to learning through openness, inclusiveness and dialogue.

COMMUNITY COMMITMENT

There is greater support from and understanding of parents and the local community, and greater willingness to participate in school development.

COLLECTIVE FOCUS ON PUPIL LEARNING

Each child's experience at school is a collective concern so that the pupil's learning experience is considered holistically.

ULTIMATE IMPROVEMENTS IN PUPIL LEARNING

A 'learning-enriched' teachers' workplace appears to be linked to increased academic progress for pupils (Rosenholtz, 1989) and in schools with positive professional communities pupils have been found to achieve at higher levels (Louis and Marks, 1998).

In the school that is a learning community, the rate of the school's learning is greater than or equal to the rate of relevant change in its environment.

> Our schools can be wonderful places of enchantment and creativity, opening doorways to new ways of perceiving, new ways of being; but they are most of all places of exquisite hope in the possibility of the future, in the possibility of people . . . this means we have to choose what is seen to matter and then go out and collectively begin to move towards achieving it.
>
> (Clarke, 2000)

The learning community's power, therefore, comes through its collective nature. It depends on people's openness to other people's ideas of the way the school operates, suspending their own judgements and assumptions. It also depends on them reaching out beyond the school into the environment as a source of important information and to the wider community as an equal partner in developing collective understanding and new knowledge. Through collective inquiry, school staff and their communities process internal or external information which challenges them to be creative in reflecting on and adapting assumptions underpinning their ways of working and leads them to new and collective ways of thinking.

Further reading and network sources

Probably the most frequently cited text on organisational learning, Peter Senge's *Fifth Discipline*, is written 'for learners, especially those of us interested in the art and practice of collective learning'. He explains how our actions create our reality, and that we have it in our power to change this. Describing 'five disciplines' of a learning organisation, he argues that it is essential that they develop as an 'ensemble'. The book has spawned several practical follow-ups by Senge and his colleagues, including *The Fifth Discipline Fieldbook, The Dance of Change* and, most recently, *Schools That Learn*.

Gareth Morgan's *Images of Organization* is a challenging but compelling read for anyone who wants to look 'outside' the box and think of their school in different ways. Analysing eight different organisational images, Morgan explains how metaphors can be powerful in creating ways of seeing and shaping organisational life, and how to integrate and use the insights of competing metaphors in managing organisations.

Profound Improvement: Building Capacity for a Learning Community, by Coral Mitchell and Larry Sackney, is an important exploration of the learning community as a vehicle for professional learning and school development, which shows how personal, interpersonal and organisational capacity fuse in schools' daily worlds.

The title *The Intelligent School* is enough to catch your attention. Using examples from schools as well as drawing on research, Barbara MacGilchrist, Kate Myers and Jane Reed pull together literature on school effectiveness and improvement, learning, effective teaching, teachers' learning and maximising pupils' progress and achievement. In the final chapter the authors adapt Howard Gardner's concept of multiple intelligences, 'putting the pieces together' to create 'the intelligent school'. A follow-up book by the same authors is in progress.

There are a number of good books on self-evaluation. We particularly like the work of John MacBeath and colleagues. The story told in *Self-Evaluation in European Schools*, from the perspective of various 'players', including a pupil, is fascinating. As a teacher told one of us, 'I loved the book – I couldn't put it down'. *Schools Must Speak for Themselves* is based on research carried out for the National Union of Teachers (NUT). Full of useful ideas, this book explains the power of self-evaluation, and offers a 'four key element' framework to support school self-evaluation: an overarching philosophy; procedural guidelines; a set of criteria or 'indicators; and a tool kit. In *Inspection: What's in it for Schools?*, James Learmonth also provides a number of international examples of school self-evaluation and suggests useful ways to blend internal and external evaluation.

Sue Askew and Eileen Carnell's *Transforming Learning: Individual and Global Change* is full of insights about learning. The authors describe transformatory learning as 'participating in the whole experience of learning'. Focusing on learners, learning contexts and learning processes, they demonstrate how emotional, social, spiritual and cognitive aspects of learning interrelate. The book also usefully highlights the importance of the group and social context on learning and how people and organisations can be transformed through engaging with the learning process.

A number of researchers in the United States have studied schools that are professional communities. Karen Seashore Louis, Sharon Kruse and Associates, in *Professionalism and Community: Perspectives on Reforming Urban Schools*, provide a framework for analysing school-based professional community. We have used this with groups of teachers and leaders to help them analyse their schools. They tell us they have found it a valuable tool.

CreativeNet (www.creativenet.org.uk) is a collaboration between Demos, the independent policy think tank, and the Design Council. Their website is 'organised around the creative process of problem solving', and encourages visitors to identify problems, immerse themselves in information, debate ideas, develop prototypes and propose solutions. This, in turn, provides 'the basis of a new inclusive method of policy development, based on practical, creative experience'.

7 Enhancing capacity for learning

For us, the way forward for schools and their larger communities is to focus hearts, minds and time on learning at all levels: pupils, teachers, leaders and the whole school as an inclusive, extended learning community. In particular, the agenda should be about all of the adults connected with schools working and learning together to support and enhance pupil learning.

> *Learning, I have always felt, is as essential as breathing.*
> Darling-Hammond (1997)

In this chapter we attempt to pull together all the pieces we have identified into a coherent whole. We start with the question: What is it that links all of these levels of learning? When learning truly permeates a school, what fuels this kind of learning? We would argue that it's the school's internal capacity: the power to get involved in and sustain the learning of everyone within the school community with the collective purpose of enhancing pupil learning (Stoll, 1999).

Philip Schlechty (2001) explains that when changes are started in systems without the capacity to sustain them, the changes are likely to disappear when the change agent leaves. Developing internal capacity depends on those both inside and outside schools.

Enhancing capacity for learning from the inside

First we look inside the school. We have identified nine themes flowing through the book that feed and nourish capacity for learning in schools. Each of these themes, or meta-learnings, provides opportunities for schools to enhance their own learning for capacity. We've used the spider's web analogy before (Stoll and Fink, 1996): if you touch one part of it, the rest reverberates because it is all interconnected (see Figure 7.1).

1 **It's about** *believing in success*

Believing you can be successful is critical to internal capacity. In the same way that Senge (1990) maintains that schools create their own reality, so does each individual in schools. If pupils, teachers and leaders do not believe in themselves and their ability to be successful in what they set out to do, they can become locked in a cycle of despair and frustration. The moving school has a pervading 'can do' culture, a belief that it is always possible to do better, no matter what difficulties it faces, and that it feels it has the power to do so. It has a learning orientation whereby people believe that effort, rather than innate ability, leads to greater success. There is no evidence of learned helplessness in such

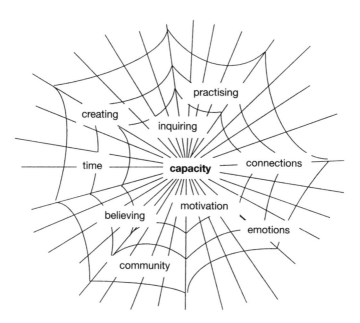

Figure 7.1 Learning for capacity

a school. Invitational leaders ensure that everyone feels valued and competent to contribute to a shared vision of a better future.

2 It's about *making connections*

Successful schools depend on connections at all levels. Connections are central to learning, and play themselves out in many forms in this book. One example is the increase in number of connections between neurons when the brain is stimulated, as shown by brain scans; in other words, new connections are added to the wiring of the brain. This finding is not limited to early development. Another example is the connection of new information to old as the learner encounters new ideas. Furthermore, experts in areas as diverse as chess, physics, maths, electronics and history notice meaningful patterns of information not noticed by novice learners, and engage in 'chunking' – connecting and organising their knowledge around important concepts (see Brandsford *et al.*, 1999). A third example is the networks that are an important feature of teachers' and leaders' learning, connecting them with other people and ideas. Fourth, there is the attention paid to patterns and interrelationships between activities and ideas as the school as a whole organisation is involved in collective learning.

3 It's about *attending to motivation*

Motivation affects people's willingness to devote time to learning. Without commitment, openness and a sense of purpose, real learning cannot take place. People may go through the motions and there may be an appearance of change but this change is likely to be shallow.

> If one is motivated to learn, one is likely to work hard, to be persistent, to be stimulated rather than discouraged by obstacles, and to continue to learn even when not pressed to do so, for the sheer pleasure of quenching curiosity or stretching one's faculties in unfamiliar directions.
>
> Gardner (1999a)

In the learning-oriented school, it is the challenge of genuine learning that is the ultimate goal, rather than purely performance or achievement.

Such learning is more likely to be lifelong because it is internally motivated: its rewards are intrinsic. It's not easily achievable and it depends on the school being focused on the needs of each learner, whatever their age and role, and oriented towards bringing out the best in all learners, individually and collectively. In short, the school is both learner-centred and learning-centred.

4 It's about *understanding and experiencing emotions*

It is clear that emotion and learning have a powerful relationship. The human dimension of learning is critical. It's not just a bonus to have good relationships in classrooms, playgrounds, staff rooms, governors' meetings and with parents: it is critical to fostering self-esteem and building the right climate for learning. Furthermore, there is a link between positive relationships between teachers and pupils and greater academic progress (Mortimore *et al.*, 1988). Some schools have therapeutic counsellors working in them, while other charities and organisations assess and provide support for at-risk pupils. On the website of Antidote, the Campaign for Emotional Literacy, Susie Orbach, the psychotherapist, explains that Antidote's aim is 'to create an emotionally literate culture, where the facility to handle the complexities of emotional life is as widespread as the capacity to read, write and do anything else'.

> *Connecting to our feelings is not soft; disconnecting from our feelings is not clever.*
>
> *Antidote website*

While some people may be right to be cynical about the dangers of managerial manipulation of emotion, the evidence from a range of sources is clear that experiencing and understanding emotions is essential to learning and to developing healthy people and society.

5 It's about *engaging in community*

Learning in schools takes place within a social context: the school community. It can be seen in co-operative learning, collaborative planning, peer observation and mentoring, leadership teams and other team work, collective learning and understanding, working parties and shared vision building. As such, it depends on positive relationships, trust and respect. At its best, it can lead to a sense of belonging to a community of learners. As Brandsford and colleagues (1999) note: '[An] important perspective on learning environments is the degree to which they promote a sense of community. Students, teachers, and other interested participants share norms that value learning and high standards. Norms such as these increase people's opportunities and motivation to interact, receive feedback, and learn.'

6 It's about *inquiring*

Learning is about needing to know, even when what you find out is something you think you didn't want to know. It means reserving judgement and being open to new ideas, gathering the necessary information, and questioning and challenging your own beliefs and perceptions. Inquiring involves such things as pupils assessing their own learning to promote deeper understanding, and teachers interrogating different ICT teaching packages to understand which ones are most likely to promote real learning and support and enhance their other learning and teaching strategies. It also involves finding out about the community in order to make the necessary and meaningful connections.

I look on losing as research, not as failure.

Billie Jean King

Where necessary, it is also about challenging the beliefs and ideas of others, rather than taking them for granted. Finally, because learning is powerfully influenced by the contexts in which it takes place – classrooms, schools, the local community, LEAs, and the national policy environment – it is imperative to understand these contexts and, where they are found to be inhibiting learning, to question and challenge them.

7 It's about creating

It concerns us if people in schools tell us there are no opportunities to create and be creative. Learning has the potential to foster creativity and creativity is an essential feature of learning as we have described it. It is also critical in a changing world. Bentley (2000) describes creativity as applying knowledge and skills in new ways to achieve a valued goal. Jaworski (1998) puts it like this: 'if individuals and organizations operate from the generative orientation, from possibility rather than resignation, we can *create* the future into which we are living, as opposed to merely reacting to it when we get there.'

A learning school is a creative school where: new ideas and taking chances are encouraged; people 'practise fearlessness' (Fullan, 1992); people feel empowered to take risks and 'think outside the box'; the aesthetic curriculum is viewed as important because of the potential it offers for the development of *learning to live together* and *learning to be*, as well as *learning to know* and *learning to do*; and the whole school community understands how it creates its own reality and has the power to change it and influence the reality of those outside.

> 'There is no use trying,' said Alice; 'one can't believe impossible things.' 'I dare say you haven't had much practice,' said the Queen. 'When I was your age, I always did it for half an hour a day. Why, sometimes I've believed as many as six impossible things before breakfast.'
>
> Lewis Carroll

8 It's about *practising*

The thing about learning is you never stop doing it. As we have argued, it requires hard work, commitment and practice. New ways of learning or creating (as the quote from Alice in Wonderland shows) don't come easily: accommodation, as a process of learning, is actually a process of coming to terms with different ideas, different ways of doing things. This usually necessitates trying something out again and again, working at it, feeling uncomfortable for a while, and experiencing new responses. With learning, however, practice doesn't make perfect – or complacent – because there is always something new to learn: as we noted in Chapter 4, a new curve and another hill.

9 It's about *finding time*

Time has been the undercurrent flowing through this book. It is impossible to argue 'It's about learning' without thinking about time.

For a range of reasons, external pressure included, learning as described in this book is not the central driving force of many schools. It's about time it was; indeed, we would argue that in the twenty-first century, it's essential. But, we also know that real change and learning are not straightforward. They depend on belief, making connections, attending to motivation, nurturing positive emotions, building community, inquiring, creating and practising, and all of this requires devotion of time. Throughout the book we have offered various ideas for creating time, but time is one of the greatest challenges for schools, especially if they are faced with teacher shortages. Time for learning and development is so important that it can't just be left to schools to find time. In the next section, we look at learnings for those outside schools.

By attending to these nine themes and by enhancing learning in the ways we have described throughout the book, you are building your school's capacity for sustainable and continuous learning.

Tony Buzan (1988), the creator of mind mapping, describes it as a form of creative note taking. The idea is to use colours, arrows and other special codes to make connections between key words, showing where relationships lie.

Take an issue in your school (or a school you know), or an initiative you want to develop. Create a mind map, putting your issue or initiative in the middle (see Figure 7.2). Track through each of the nine themes in this book, asking yourselves, for example: 'What does this mean for community?' 'How do we go about creating community in relation to this?' 'What are the forces working in our favour and preventing us from harnessing community to its fullest in relation to this issue/initiative?' 'How can we draw on the positive forces and reduce the negative forces?'

Enhancing capacity for learning from the outside

Having identified nine avenues for enhancing capacity from the inside, we now turn to enhancing capacity from outside schools. We have argued in this book that schools have the power to enhance their own learning. Our research and experience working in and with schools, however, also tells us that they can't do it alone.

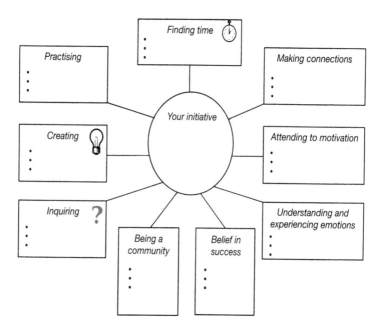

Figure 7.2 Mind map of your initiative

At the Fourteenth International Congress for School Effectiveness and Improvement in Toronto in January 2001, practitioners, local and national policy makers, researchers, non-government organisations and consultants representing 43 countries came together to discuss issues of equity, globalisation and change. A recurring theme was the importance of schools' local, national and, indeed, international context and, particularly, the role of the system in helping or hindering schools' ability to learn. Central external influences on schools' capacity for learning (Stoll, 1999 – see Figure 7.3) are:

- Their *local communities*. Pupils' background characteristics influence their schools' achievement, and parental expectations and aspirations often vary according to the type and location of school.
- The *broader community* (e.g. business, media, unions, university, etc.) and the expectations it has of them.

- *Political action and 'tone'* – teachers bombarded by unrelenting change can feel guilty, get exhausted, and find it hard to maintain energy, enthusiasm and willingness for change. Labelling 'failing schools' can also exacerbate problems of schools in difficulty, contributing to low morale and feelings of impotence.
- Whether the *professional learning infrastructure* in their area or region is well developed, for example access to outside ideas, universities, centres of school development, etc.
- The *global change forces* described at the start of the book shaping schools' daily existence, making it imperative that schools have the internal capacity to respond to such forces.

Some people maintain that schools need to be challenged to change. At times, this may be true for some schools, for example the cruising school. Unequivocally, however, to become and remain successful learning communities, and to improve learning standards, all schools

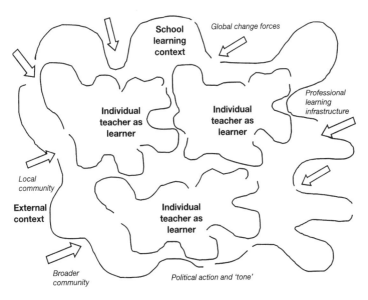

Figure 7.3 External influences on schools' capacity for learning

Source: Based on Stoll (1999)

require external support. Alma Harris (2001) describes this external capacity building as being 'concerned with creating the conditions, opportunities and experiences for collaboration and mutual learning'. This includes equitably and purposefully distributing resources: not only monetary resources but human, material and psychological support and, of course, time. Essentially, schools need an infrastructure of support from all groups with a responsibility for or interest in school improvement to develop capacity. Throughout this book we have proposed learnings for those located within schools. We also believe that there are learnings for those outside schools to take on board in order to provide the necessary learning support infrastructure. Here we propose eight learnings for schools' learning partners, including parents and carers, governors, the local community, LEAs, businesses, unions and associations, universities, and the government. These are different kinds of partners: some of them provide political support, some professional support, and others moral and emotional support. Some provide a combination of support. We have not differentiated our learnings for the different partners because we believe that all partners need to understand the breadth of external support needed.

1 Recognise the importance of learning for all

We are all learning for a different world. In this changed world schools can no longer afford to be sorting institutions to determine who can and cannot learn. They must be learning communities for one and all. Parents, quite justifiably, want the best for their own children. They also want their children to live in a world free of war, hunger and fear. As the world becomes more complex, it is in societies' best interest to have well-educated citizens. It is important for the public to support the improvement of *all* schools and help enhance their capacity for learning as a way of keeping the culture strong and prepared for an uncertain future. Teaching and learning aren't just up to teachers, support staff and leaders in schools. There is a collective external responsibility as well: it will take a concerted effort on everyone's part.

Learning provides hope. At the ICSEI conference in Toronto, Stephen Lewis, Canada's former ambassador to the United Nations, described recent trips to Rwanda. He told his audience that what struck him so forcefully was that wherever he went, no matter how adverse the conditions, when he asked what was important to children the answer was school. When one of us worked in Hungary with largely eastern European teams supported by the Open Society Institute, we were given a book of poems written by children at the height of the conflict in Sarajevo. One, in particular, left a lasting impression.

'HELLO MY FRIEND!'

My name is Mirela
I am seven years old girl.
My mother, father and old brother and sister are with me in Sarajevo, the capital of Bosnia and Herzegovina
We are captured in our town. It was a very nice old town, which is destroyed now. We haven't food, fruit, water, electric . . .
We haven't happy childhood.
Children don't want the war.
My friend and me have our way to fight against the war.
We learn.
Best regards.

Mirela

Open Society Fund (1994)

While there are common elements to learning, as we have noted, people bring their unique differences to the learning process. This means that, whether you are thinking about pupils, teachers, other support staff, leaders, parents or anyone else, the keys to unlocking and enhancing the learning process vary from individual to individual. Just because something worked for you when you were at school, it doesn't mean that this will be right for all learners or for the current times. The importance of learning for all also includes the ongoing learning of those outside schools, whether through one's local school, as described in Chapter 6, being enrolled in adult education or Open University courses, or attending family learning weekends. As Andy Hargreaves and Michael Fullan (1998) assert, educational partnerships 'must be actively committed to social justice by agitating for changes that favour all students, not just the highest achieving or more privileged ones who promise the biggest success and corporate return'.

2 *Respect and promote professionalism*

We have argued that being a teacher today includes more than teaching and related responsibilities. It also means: working with others as part of a larger learning community; being collectively responsible for all pupils, engaging parents, carers and the community in meaningful, and sometimes different, ways; taking personal responsibility for continuing professional development, supported by the school; and being inquiry-oriented. If this is necessary for teachers in today's world, then teachers need to be afforded the respect that accompanies such demanding and important responsibilities.

In 1998 Andy Hargreaves and Michael Fullan 'told society' that 'until it realizes that the quality and morale of teachers is absolutely central to the well-being of students and their learning, all serious reform efforts are bound to fail'. Teachers' conditions of service are critical. It is encouraging to hear of schemes to increase teachers' pay and help them pay back student loans, but if teachers do not feel valued, this significantly reduces the impact of increased pay or, for that matter, any other incentives. Pay has been found to be a relatively unimportant factor in relation to teacher morale, motivation and job satisfaction (Evans, 1998), which is not to say that teachers are adequately paid for their work.

Teachers, however, need time to learn and implement their learning, assess and evaluate, plan, and collaborate with colleagues, parents and others. They also need funded learning and administrative support so that they can focus on enhancing pupil learning. Most important, they need recognition that they are doing a good job, particularly those who work in challenging areas. Award and other merit schemes for teachers provide one kind of recognition, but teachers also feel recognition from direct contact with satisfied parents, letters from former pupils thanking them for making a difference, and small but significant successes on a daily basis. In stark contrast, blame, from whatever source, doesn't reach the 'hearts and minds' of those needing to be reached for change to occur (Stoll and Myers, 1998).

Supporting and promoting professionalism may also require a greater focus of unions' energies around the professional aspects of teachers' work that enhance learning. There are already many positive examples, including support for a study of school self-evaluation in England (Bangs,

2000; MacBeath *et al.*, 1996), conferences run by professional associations on topics such as 'Why Learn?' (Association of Teachers and Lecturers, 1996), support of unions for schemes such as Investors in People, and the development by the National Education Association in the USA of a data-driven local school improvement process called KEYS (NEA, 1996). Louis and colleagues (2000) note that this 'new unionism', as they describe it, requires systemic effort: resources, individual advocates, and leadership, as well as efforts to encourage and reward locally initiated change and re-educate the membership. They conclude: 'It will also require patience and time if we are to see the benefits of new unionism in improved schools and learning opportunities for students.'

3 Support continuous professional learning

All professions need to invest in development. Continuous learning is every teacher's, leader's and support person's business, but they can't be expected to do it on their own. In his foreword to *Learning and Teaching*, the document outlining the government's strategy for professional development (DfEE, 2001), David Blunkett, then Secretary of State for Education, in writing about the challenges and pressures brought about by change, concluded: 'it is necessary to offer the maximum support to teachers in achieving the highest standards possible, and taking on this challenge of change'. A variety of funded initiatives are aimed at developing, enhancing and sharing excellent practice and placing professional development 'at the heart of schools improvement'. The initiatives include: research scholarships, international study visits, professional bursaries, sabbaticals for teachers (particularly those working in deprived areas) early professional development for teachers in their second and third years of teaching, and individual learning accounts, where for a small personal investment, teachers can get discounts off learning and development opportunities.

If systems to support professional growth are intended to sustain their learning, they must, however, help schools develop as learning communities where educators collaborate to enquire critically about their own practice. Encouragingly, the national strategy recognises the importance of the school as a learning community, and aims to provide increased time for whole staffs to work together developing their learning community.

The National Staff Development Council in the USA has worked with a large number of national associations and many individuals to create consensus on the kinds of staff development that ensure that all students and staff are learning and performing at high levels (Hirsch, 2001). Their 12 standards for staff development are grouped in three categories, all of which are prefaced by the phrase 'Staff development that improves the learning of all students':

- **Context** – where adults are grouped into *learning communities*; with school and external *leadership* to guide continuous improvement; and *resources* to support adult learning and collaboration.
- **Process** – where adult learning priorities, progress and sustained improvement are *data-driven*; *evaluation* guides improvement and demonstrates the impact of staff development; educators learn how to make *research-based* decisions; *design* of learning strategies is appropriate to the intended goal; knowledge about human *learning* and change is applied; and educators are provided with knowledge and skills for *collaboration*.
- **Content** – where concerns about *equity* ensure educators are prepared to understand and appreciate all students, holding high expectations for their achievement; *quality teaching* is emphasised through deepening of content knowledge and use of research-based learning, teaching and assessment strategies; and educators are provided with knowledge and skills for enhancing *family involvement*, as well as that of other stakeholders.

4 Get to know your school(s)

Essentially, the best way to know how to support a school is to get to know it. This means learning about it. Can a school's local community answer the question, 'How good is your local school, really?' (Stoll, 2001). There is a lot of information around about schools, but some of it may just be folklore. Other information, such as league tables of results, may not take into account the background of the pupils who attend the school and the actual value the school has added. Schools receive considerable data from the DfES and, where relevant, the LEA to help them understand the school. Many also now ask their pupils to complete questionnaires on their attitudes to learning and school and their academic self-concept. Schools also produce newsletters and handbooks that describe their programmes, successes and preferred futures. These are helpful indicators that aren't found in league tables.

Other qualitative indicators may be picked up by visiting schools, watching lessons and offering assistance, for example listening to pupils read or helping them with ICT during their lunch break. As outsiders consider what they read, see and hear, they may want to ask themselves to what extent this evidence suggests that the school is a learning community.

5 Understand that all schools are not the same

If you get to know schools, it won't take very long to realise that they are all different from each other. Schools embark on their learning journeys from very different starting points; indeed, some find it enormously difficult to get off the starting block. This, we believe, is because of differences in their internal capacity: some schools are more 'ready' than others to deal with and work through the challenges associated with learning. They have the resources, resilience and will to engage in and sustain continuous learning of teachers, leaders and the school itself, and have a clear vision of its primary purpose as enhancing pupil learning.

As we have described, influences on a school's internal capacity operate at the individual teacher and leader level, the school level (and, in secondary schools, also at department or faculty level) and external level. The capacity of schools differs as a result of different patterns of influences. For example, schools differ in terms of their leadership, motivation, prior learning experiences, support infrastructure, and particular blend of pupils. Finding out particular patterns of influences on a school's internal capacity is essential because these influence the school's readiness to engage in learning as well as its ability to sustain learning and enhance learning outcomes over time. Schools also exist within a wider social context, and disadvantage has a significant impact on schools (Mortimore and Whitty, 1997). As results are coming through on the mapping of the human genome, and we hear that humans have far fewer genes than previously expected (estimates suggest between 30,000 and 40,000), the influence of social context may assume even greater importance.

It is vital to vary learning support strategies for different schools. What works in one school, with a particular pupil population and at a particular stage of development, may not work in another. A cruising school in an affluent leafy suburb has different learning and development needs from a struggling school in the inner city, and that latter school may have different needs from a struggling school in an area of rural deprivation. Certain government initiatives already take context into account, for example Excellence in Cities. Others take more of a blanket approach to improvement, although it is encouraging to see increasing recognition of the importance of school differences. Some schools have greater need for extra external resources and support, while others may need greater external pressure for change, and they may not always be the schools highlighted by the media as schools in difficulty. Fullan (1999) argues: 'there never will be a definitive theory of change. It is a theoretical and empirical impossibility to generate a theory that applies to all situations . . . each situation will have degrees of uniqueness in its history and makeup which will cause unpredictable differences to emerge.'

Schools in disadvantaged areas, in particular, need co-ordinated support strategies involving education, health and social services agencies working with local communities and school psychologists. One such example is the Healthier Schools Partnership, started in three London boroughs, Lewisham, Lambeth and Southwark, which has now been extended nationally.

A collaborative three-year programme involving Essex LEA's development advisors, educational psychologists and special needs support service, the University of Cambridge School of Education, and 22 primary and junior schools highlighted several important lessons for the working practices of multi-disciplinary teams (Kerfoot and Nethercott, 1999). These were:

- time for teams to develop mutual respect and confidence in each other
- secure individual knowledge
- the professional confidence of a range of school staff
- complementary skills with clearly defined roles, negotiated and accepted by all
- ability to network and provide perspectives on an issue

- a clear team focus
- support and challenge appropriate to the school's context
- schools having the primary responsibility for their own development
- the team bringing in 'added' value that is clearly defined, supports, complements and, when appropriate, challenges
- a 'mature' approach to problem solving, based on a recognition and confidence from each individual in their own knowledge, skills and contribution, shared with others as well as received.

6 Create new designs for working with and networking schools

We hope we have made it clear that learning in schools depends on many different things coming together. Research has been useful in highlighting the different conditions under which schools are likely to improve (see Hopkins, 2001a for a summary). It has also provided evidence on successful approaches to enhancing pupils' learning in a range of subjects (e.g. Marie Clay's work on *Reading Recovery*, 1993). Over a number of years there has been an emergence of 'design' programmes in different countries. Peter Hill and colleagues in Australia describe these as taking a more holistic approach to change and learning than just emphasising the specific change focus. For example, in Victoria, schools participating in their Middle Years Research and Development (MYRAD) project don't just study and develop appropriate strategies for teaching adolescents; they also pay equal attention to a range of conditions related to improved learning outcomes (Hill and Russell, 1999 – see Figure 7.4).

Similarly, elementary (primary) schools involved in Chicago's Center for School Improvement's School Development Program, while focusing on literacy as their key lever for change, all pay attention to:

a myriad of concerns that impinge upon children's well being and ultimately their learning. These include: renorming the school environment to educate and care for all children; coordinating and managing academic and social services so that students' social, physical, health, and emotional needs are better met; strengthening school community leadership to broaden participation and sustain

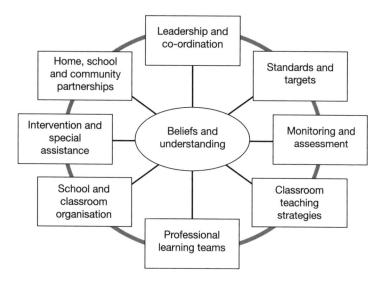

Figure 7.4 Whole-school design model for school improvement
Source: Hill and Crévola (1997)

a focus on the needs of children; and building the analytic capacities within schools to engage in continual improvement.

(Bryk *et al.*, 1996)

Perhaps the best-known example currently in England is the Improving the Quality of Education for All (IQEA) programme (Hopkins, 2001b; Hopkins *et al.*, 1994), a network of schools, supported by colleagues in a range of universities and by their LEAs. The IQEA team identified a set of enabling school-level conditions for school development – staff development; involvement; 'transformational' leadership; effective co-ordination; enquiry and reflection; and collaborative planning – and a complementary set of classroom conditions – authentic relationships; rules and boundaries; planning, resources and preparation; a broad and appropriate teaching repertoire; pedagogic partnerships; and reflection on teaching.

All the elements in a learning-centred school are interrelated and, as Clive Dimmock (2000) explains, 'the design needs built-in flexibility for continuous evolution and adaptability in fast changing environments'. Dimmock also highlights the need to emphasise the interconnections between all parts of a school, and that no single blueprint of school design is appropriate for all schools, despite general approaches which can provide guidelines.

Networking is increasingly being seen as vital to extending and deepening teachers', support staff's and leaders' learning (Lieberman and Grolnick, 1996; Stoll, 1996; Earl and Lee, 1998). One of us established a school improvement network, bringing together people engaged in school improvement to share and discuss experiences, debate issues of mutual concern, reflect on their learning, solve common problems and further refine improvement strategies (Stoll, 1996). The National Writing Project (NWP) in the USA is based on the notion that teaching requires a continuous circle of learning, trial and evaluation. Teachers articulate their own dilemmas and find ways to resolve these. Through regional and national networks, as teachers are working on their local problems, they reach beyond their schools to connect with other teachers, give and receive ideas, support and critique. In their evaluation of NWP, Lieberman and Wood (2001) found that 'by connecting learning, community, and efficacy, NWP provides teachers with a variety of opportunities not only to shape ideas for use in their own contexts, but to take leadership in and become members of a larger professional community'. Some of the specific ways in which teachers learn in this network are by:

- teaching other teachers
- making their work public and having it discussed and critiqued by a group of peers
- agreeing that feedback from colleagues will be non-judgmental and non-ideological, even if views about issues such as phonics or whole language are different
- learning to accept and discuss openly the 'messiness' and 'uncertainty' of teaching, which is often dealt with privately by teachers
- taking different roles and seeing the world through different perspectives
- taking leadership learning back to their peers in their school, by setting up similar environments for them.

7 Offer critical friendship

People within schools don't always see everything that is going on. External eyes can often pick up what is not immediately apparent to those inside a school. Critical friends are people who watch, listen, ask challenging questions, and help those in schools sort out their thinking and make sound decisions. Sometimes they help by providing coaching support. What is particularly important to this relationship is that it is one built on trust and support: critical friends don't bring their own vested interests. They will, however, tell people in the school when they consider that expectations are too low or interpretations are 'off track'. Such difficult messages – while uncomfortable and, sometimes, painful to hear – are more likely to be accepted and addressed because those in the school know that the critical friend is fundamentally 'on their side'. This requires enormous sensitivity and diplomacy on the part of the critical friend.

An example of this can be seen in the comments of a headteacher of a primary school in the ISEP project, describing the benefits of their critical friend:

> He appeared to value each individual situation and what each person had to offer to that situation . . . He helped us to keep focused and positive about the situation here. After the initial results the staff morale in the school sank and the staff were zonked. The critical friend quickly brought us back to looking at the positives and look at what we were actually doing and not at what we were not doing . . . He helped us to be reflective, how we could improve our own practice . . . He was not judgmental . . . He respected people's point of view.

Critical friends' work changes over time. For example, sustaining improvement is particularly challenging. After the catalyst promoting the decision to change, there is a surge of energy as people become actively involved in the early stages (Earl and Lee, 1998 – see Figure 7.5).

Initial 'excitement', however, wears off as teachers are faced with other demands, as well as inevitable difficulties presented by both the innovation and the school's internal capacity: for example, overload, complexity, internal power struggles, or an impending inspection. The

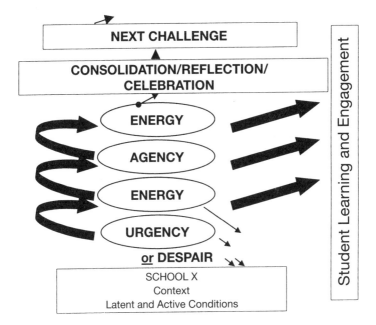

Figure 7.5 Spiral of school improvement

Source: Earl and Lee (1998)

school, or at least the intended improvement focus, faces turbulence (Huberman, 1992) and without 'agency' – internal resources or access to appropriate and timely support (Earl and Lee, 2000) – change may be modest and uninspiring. The critical friend needs to know how to vary the relationship and provide the right support at different times.

The Improving School Effectiveness Project (ISEP) distinguished phases of the relationship as critical friends work in schools (Doherty *et al.*, 2001).

INITIAL CONTACT

Early stages are important times for establishing ground rules for future operations, agreeing broad parameters within which the school and critical friend will work and, particularly, creating a 'mutual comfort zone'. Developing a spirit of trust is important in enabling people to speak openly and share thoughts, ideas and concerns with others. Listening, openness and availability all feature in developing such a trusting relationship.

THE FIRST HURDLE

Feeding back data can be a sensitive task, but the situation is eased if critical friends are totally familiar with the data and comfortable with handling it and its interpretation within the particular school's context. After being presented with data, a few ISEP schools were reluctant to continue their involvement with the process. Attempts were then made 'to enter the school by "another door"'. It is important to explain data clearly and unambiguously, leaving no room for confusion. Furthermore, valid interpretation is necessary, to enable schools to see the realities of their own situations objectively. This requires careful listening, reflecting on issues raised, reformulating interpretations, picking out positive aspects, and encouraging people to reflect on how these can be built on.

WHERE NEXT?

Most notably, this is the time when the critical friend begins to move from the role of friend to that of critic. There isn't one pattern for working with all schools, or a single path to take. It depends on each school's comfort level and readiness for change. Respect for individual confidentiality continues to be important at this stage, as is the ability to: help others to self-evaluate; present examples from elsewhere in such a way that teachers can reflect on the relative merits of each; challenge people to broaden and extend their self-perception; 'referee' discussions; encourage, praise, clarify and revisit issues to help people maintain momentum; and, where necessary, play the role of confidant(e). In all they do, more effective critical friends are aware that they need to leave schools more self-sufficient in their own learning processes. In moving towards disengaging from the school, the critical friend helps people move to a reflective, dialogic approach that incorporates greater openness to questioning and a respect for evidence: 'The question "how do you know?" eventually ceases to be put by the critical friend and becomes a routine way of thinking' (MacBeath, 1998a).

John MacBeath has summarised the formal and informal aspects of the critical friend's agenda (see Table 7.1).

Coaching can be seen as one form of critical friendship and is also a valuable form of support for schools, particularly school leaders. While sports coaches may have a very clear strategy or game plan for their team to execute, the kind of coaching we are referring to is one where the 'client' – the school or particular person within the school – decides

Table 7.1 Critical friend's agenda

Formal	*Informal*
Introduction Clarifying roles, agreeing parameters	*Background reading* Documents, contextual information, getting to know the school
Gathering data Interviews, observation, group activities	*Familiarization* Making contacts with staff and pupils, building, confidence
Organizing data Making sense of and systematizing data	*Negotiating a role* Establishing style, listening mode
Feeding back data Building alliances	*Building alliances* Moving out of the comfort zone, beyond the management team
Making sense of data Helping the school to understand and define issues	*Facilitating* Entering into discussion, raising questions, offering suggestions
Considering the options Working within the school's agenda, planning priorities, target setting	*Monitoring* Reflecting on actions taken, evaluating self; record-keeping, reviewing
Supporting initiatives Sitting in on working groups, working alongside teachers (e.g. co-operative teaching)	*Challenging* Broadening and extending the school's self perception
Embedding Helping to develop structures and procedures to sustain long term growth	*Maintaining momentum* Encouraging, praising, clarifying, revisiting issues
Evaluating Identifying achievement	*Disengaging* Removing crutches

Source: MacBeath (1998a)

> *Coaching is unlocking a person's potential to maximize their own performance. It is helping them to learn rather than teaching them.*
>
> *Whitmore (1996)*

on their own agenda. Jenny Rogers (2001) endorses the need for coaching to start and finish with the client's agenda: 'This is because coaching is about change', and we have already highlighted that change involves motivation. If change really is to come from within (Barth, 1990) then those in schools really have to want to change.

Ultimately, the most effective critical friendship helps a school enhance its own learning, as was discovered by the Improving School Effectiveness Project in Scotland (MacBeath and Mortimore, 2001), in which one of us was involved: 'There is one touchstone question for the critical friend, which is not too far away from what a teacher would, or should, ask in relation to the class or individual learner: "Will this help to develop independence, the capacity to learn and to apply learning more effectively over time?"' (MacBeath, 1998a). Such friendships are critical.

8 Time for deep learning

We have shown that deep and meaningful learning is complex. You can have higher expectations of pupils and offer them greater support, but if the back-up home support isn't there, it will take longer, and sometimes the most dramatic changes aren't seen for a while.

Dick (1992) poses a question about Chinese bamboo: 'When you plant it nothing happens in the first year, nor in the second or the third or the fourth years. You don't even see a single green shoot. And yet in the fifth year, in a space of just six weeks, the bamboo will grow 90 feet high. The question is, did it grow 90 feet in six weeks or in five years?'

In response to the social forces we described in our introductory chapter, policy makers throughout the world have initiated dramatic – indeed some might say revolutionary – changes in state-supported education. What has emerged is what Hargreaves, Earl and colleagues (2001) have called 'the new educational orthodoxy'. This 'new orthodoxy' advocates higher standards of learning, deeper learning, centralised and often standardised curriculum, a focus on basics such as literacy and numeracy, and accountability procedures that drive teaching and teachers practice. In practice, however, there is considerable evidence (Fielding, 2001a; Hargreaves *et al.*, 2001; Tye, 2000) that 'the new orthodoxy' can create fragmented, 'hurried' (Elkind, 1997) curricula unresponsive to differences in children and contexts. Rather than deeper learning it can create pressures on teachers and pupils to cover volumes of often undigested content to meet the requirements of tests and exams. Judith Warren Little (2001) explains how 'Reform environments tend to be volatile, fast-paced, and public, while learning may require sustained concentration, gradual development, and opportunities for relatively private ("safe") disclosure of struggles and uncertainties'. Perhaps a rather linear, technicist approach to educational change may be a necessary stage in the evolution of educational systems and schools towards the 'deep' kind of learning that this book advocates. The second meaning of our title is that *it is about time* that systems and schools move beyond the 'new orthodoxy' to embrace 'deep' learning for understanding. As Hargreaves and Fink (2000) state:

> Increasingly, educational reformers want more than improved achievement results of any kind. They want deep, powerful, high performance learning-for-understanding that prepares young people to participate in today's knowledge or informational society.
>
> Learning for understanding is not just a cognitive and psychological matter, though. It involves more than constructivism, multiple intelligences, metacognition, or problem-based learning. Deep learning and teaching are also cultural and emotional processes. They entail contextualizing students' learning in what they have learned before, in what other teachers are also teaching them, and in students' own cultures and lives. This deep contextualization of learning which gets students engaged in it, is a cultural and not just a cognitive task.

It may be possible to change teachers' behaviour by making them do things in different ways. Nonetheless, even if they can be persuaded that the change is worthwhile and makes a positive difference (which is not always guaranteed), bringing about that change is hard work. Given the complexity and challenge of learning, it is critical that all interested stakeholders, whether parents or the broader community including politicians, respect that such development can't occur without a significant investment of time. For pupils this means time for them and their teachers to explore ideas in depth rather than rushing through a crowded curriculum. It also means time for them to gain an emotional as well as a cognitive understanding of their new learning (Hargreaves and Fink, 2000). It means less testing time and more time for assessment *for* learning. It also means parents devoting time to their children's learning, through reading with them, talking with them and discussing ideas, and taking them to places they haven't been before. For teachers it includes:

- planning time
- time for learning new teaching techniques, and particularly time for processing and integrating learning from professional development experiences
- time for observing lessons by peers and trying out new practices
- time for researching one's own practice
- time for reviewing data and ideas, reflecting, arguing and clarifying the next steps
- time for working collectively and creatively as a whole school community to ensure that each pupil's learning is as enriching as it can possibly be.

It also means that external consultants supporting schools, whether university- or LEA-based or freelance, need to be able to offer 'just in time' support (Earl and Lee, 1998) that matches the needs of schools and their stage of development, and leads to deep learning.

> Speed is a defence against depth and meaning. Nothing important happens quickly. Choose quality of experience over speed. The world changes from depth of commitment and capacity to learn.
>
> Block *et al.* (2000)

Earlier in this chapter we indicated that the external learnings were for all stakeholders outside schools. Policy makers, however, have a unique and powerful opportunity to shape the support infrastructure for learning. We suggest that it is time to look beyond the 'new orthodoxy' to an educational system truly built around learning. To this end we offer the following policy suggestions:

- Define curriculum in terms of learnings, not subjects, and empower schools to address these learnings across the school. We recommend that the organisation and at least 30 per cent of the curriculum be designed locally to respond to the contextual needs of different communities.
- Design assessments that assess pupils' learning in authentic ways. If the number and volume of national assessments is reduced, resources can be mobilised to 'evaluate what is valued'.
- Develop inspection systems that provide support, guidance and critical friendship (Learmonth, 2000).
- Build teachers' and leaders' professional development around sets of learnings such as those described in Chapters 4 and 5. While ongoing professional learning shouldn't be optional for teachers and leaders, they should be able to exercise considerable professional discretion in determining how they achieve these learnings.
- Invest in significant dedicated professional learning time as a vital prerequisite to achieve vibrant learning communities. Invest in long-term sustainable capacity building for all schools rather than 'quick fixes' and short-term expedients (Stoll and Myers, 1998).

Create a second mind map, again placing the school's issue/ initiative in the centre. This time work through each of the external learnings that would need to be in place to support the school's learning. Ask yourselves similar questions to the previous mind map questions.

It really is about time

For anyone who thinks we are just a bunch of idealists and 'it's about time' we got real and remembered the constraints and pressure people work under in schools, we do. We'll reiterate a story we've told before of the parent complaining to the teacher on parent's night about the new ways of learning in schools. The sub-text here was 'Why isn't it more like the way I was taught in school? It worked fine for me' (although this parent may not remember or know that it didn't 'work fine' for a number of his peers). The teacher replied: 'I have a choice. I can either prepare your child for your past or her future. Which would you prefer?' Making these choices means deciding what you will give up doing as well as what you will start or keep on doing.

For anyone who thinks we think that what we are suggesting is easy to do, we don't. Learning is extremely hard. It takes energy, commitment and openness, and requires the support of other learners. But it is also hopeful, forward looking, and gives us all the best way of trying to create our 'preferred futures'. After a primary headteachers' conference at which she spoke, a head came up to one of us. 'I'm going to send you a poem I've read to the kids at assembly,' she said. 'I think it captures what you've been saying to us.' We do too.

'The Door'

Go and open the door.
> Maybe outside there's
> a tree, or a wood,
> a garden,
> or a magic city.

Go and open the door.
> Maybe a dog's rummaging.
> Maybe you'll see a face,
or an eye,
or the picture
>> of a picture.

Go and open the door.
> If there's a fog
> it will clear.

Go and open the door.
> Even if there's only
> the darkness ticking,
> even if there's only
> the hollow wind,
> even if
>> nothing
>>> is there,

go and open the door.

At least
there'll be
a draught.

Miroslav Holub
(Trans. Ian Milner and George Theiner)

Learning is about enhancing our capacity for a complex and changing future and it's about time we took this seriously so each of us can learn *to know*, *to do*, *to live* and *to be*, and help young people do the same. That's what's really in it for schools.

References

Abbott, J. and Ryan, T. (2000) *The Unfinished Revolution: Learning, Human Behaviour, Community and Political Paradox*. Stafford: Network Educational Press.

Adelman, N. E. and Walking-Eagle, K. P. (1997) Teachers, Time and School Reform, in A. Hargreaves (ed.) *Rethinking Educational Change with Heart and Mind* (1997 ASCD Yearbook). Alexandria, VA: ASCD.

Adey, P. and Shayer, M. (1994) *Really Raising Standards: Cognitive Intervention and Academic Achievement*. London: Routledge.

American Psychological Association Presidential Task Force on Psychology in Education (1993) *Learner-centered Psychological Principles: Guidelines for School Redesign and Reform*. Washington, DC: APA and Mid-Continent Regional Educational Laboratory.

Ames, C. (1992) Classrooms: goals, structures and student motivation, *Journal of Educational Psychology*, 84 (3): 261–71.

Argyris, C. and Schön, D. (1978) *Organizational Learning: A Theory of Action Perspective*. Reading, MA: Addison-Wesley.

Armstrong, T. (1994) *Multiple Intelligences in the Classroom*. Alexandria, VA: ASCD.

Armstrong, T. (1998) *Awakening Genius in the Classroom*. Alexandria, VA: ASCD.

Arnold, J., Cooper, C. L. and Robertson, I. T. (1998) *Work Psychology: Understanding Human Behaviour in the Workplace*. Harlow, Essex: Financial Times/Prentice Hall.

Ashton, P., Hunt, P., Jones, P. and Watson, Y. (1981) *The Curriculum in Action*, Course PE 234. Milton Keynes: Open University Press.

Ashworth, A. (1998) *Once in a House on Fire*. London: Picador.

Askew, M., Brown, M., Rhodes, V., Johnson, D. and Wiliam, D. (1997) *Effective Teachers of Numeracy*. Final Report to the TTA. London: Kings College School of Education.

Askew, S. and Carnell, E. (1998) *Transforming Learning: Individual and Global Change*. London: Cassell.

Assessment Reform Group (1999) *Assessment for Learning: Beyond the Black Box*, Cambridge: University of Cambridge School of Education.

Association of Teachers and Lecturers (1996) *Why Learn? Report of an ATL Education Conference*. London: ATL.

Ball, S. (1987) *Micropolitics of the School*. London: Methuen.

Ball, D. L. and Cohen, D. K. (1999) Developing Practice, Developing Practitioners: Towards a Practice-based Theory of Professional Education, in L. Darling-Hammond and G. Sykes (eds) *Teaching as a Learning Profession: Handbook of Policy and Practice*. San Francisco: Jossey-Bass.

Bangs, J. (2000) Bringing Teacher Organisations Back into the Frame, in K. A. Riley and K. S. Louis (eds) *Leadership for Change and School Reform; International Perspectives*. London: RoutledgeFalmer.

Barber, B. (1995) *Jihad vs. McWorld: How Globalism and Tribalism are Reshaping the World*. New York: Ballentine Books.

Barth, R. (1990) *Improving Schools from Within: Teachers, Parents and Principals Can Make the Difference*. San Francisco: Jossey-Bass.

Barth, R. (2001) *Learning by Heart*. San Francisco: Jossey-Bass.

Battistich, V., Solomon, D., Kim, D., Watson, M. and Schaps, E. (1995) Schools as communities, poverty levels of student populations, and students' attitudes, motives, and performance: a multilevel analysis, *American Education Research Journal*, 32: 627–58.

Bayliss, V. (1999) *Opening Minds: Education for the 21st Century*. London: RSA.

Beare, H. (1996) *Trends for Global Citizenship, for the World of Work, and for Personal Formation*. Jolimont, VA: IARTV.

Beare, H. (2001) *Creating the Future School*. London: RoutledgeFalmer.

Bennis, W. and Nanus, B. (1985). *Leaders*. New York: Harper & Row.

Bentley, T. (2000) Learning for a Creative Age, in P. Crake (ed.) *Education Futures: Lifelong Learning*. London: RSA and Design Council.

Biggs, J. B. and Moore, P. J. (1993) *The Process of Learning*. 3rd edition. Englewood Cliffs, NJ: Prentice-Hall.

Bishop, K. and Denley, P. (1997) *Effective Learning in Science*. Stafford: Network Educational Press.

Black, P. and Wiliam, D. (1998a) Assessment and classroom learning, *Assessment in Education*, 5 (1): 7–74.

Black, P. and Wiliam, D. (1998b) *Inside the Black Box: Raising Standards Through Classroom Assessment*. London: Kings College School of Education.

Blase, J. (1998) The Micropolitics of Educational Change, in A. Hargreaves, A. Lieberman, M. Fullan and D. Hopkins (1998) *International Handbook of Educational Change*. Dordrecht, Netherlands: Kluwer Press.

Block, P. (1993) *Stewardship: Choosing Service Over Self Interest*. San Francisco: Berrett Kohler.

Block, P. (2000) *Flawless Consulting: A Guide to Getting Your Expertise Used*. 2nd edition. San Francisco: Jossey-Bass Pfeiffer.

Block, P. and 30 Flawless Consultants, assisted by Markovik, A. M. (2000) *The Flawless Consulting Fieldbook Companion: A Guide to Understanding Your Expertise*. San Francisco: Jossey-Bass Pfeiffer.

Bohm, D. (1985) *Unfolding Meaning*. New York: Doubleday.

Bolam, R., McMahon, A., Pocklington, K. and Weindling, D. (1995) Mentoring for new headteachers: recent British experience, *Journal of Educational Administration*, 33 (5): 29–44.

Bolman, L. and Deal, T. (1997) *Reframing Organizations: Artistry, Choice and Leadership*. 2nd edition. San Francisco: Jossey-Bass.

Bouchikhi, H. and Kimberly, J. R. (2000) The Customized Workplace, in S. Chowdhury (ed.) *Management 21C: New Visions for the New Millennium*. Harlow, Essex: Finanical Times/Prentice Hall.

Brandsford, J. D., Brown, A. L. and Cocking, R. R. (1999) *How People Learn: Brain, Mind, Experience, and School*. Washington, DC: National Academy Press.

Broadfoot, P. (1996) Liberating the Learner Through Assessment, in G. Claxton, T. Atkinson, M. Osborn and M. Wallace (eds) *Liberating the Learner*. London: Routledge.

Broadfoot, P., Claxton, G. and Deakin Crick, R. (2001) *The Challenge of Assessing Learning Power: Developing an IQ Test for the 21st Century*. Paper presented to the 27th Annual International Association for Educational Assessment Conference. Rio de Janeiro, Brazil, May.

Brophy, J. E. (1998) *Motivating Students to Learn*. Boston: McGraw-Hill.

Brophy, J. E. and Good, T. L. (1970) Teachers' communication of differential expectations for children's classroom performance: some behavioral data, *Journal of Educational Psychology*, 61 (3): 365–74.

Brown, P. and Lauder, H. (2001) *Capitalism and Social Progress: The Future of Society in a Global Economy*. Basingstoke, Hampshire: Palgrave.

Browne, A. (2001) Antidote to the stiff upper lip, *Observer*, 21 January, p. 11.

Bruner, J. and Haste, H. (1987) *Making Sense: The Child's Construction of the World*. London: Methuen.

Bryk, A. S., Rollow, S. G., and Pinnell, G. S. (1996) Urban school development: literacy as a lever for change, *Educational Policy*, 10 (2): 172–201.

Bryk, A., Sebring, P., Rollow, S. and Easton, J. (1998). *Charting Chicago School Reform*. Boulder, CO: Westview Press.

Bullock, K. and Wikeley, F. (2001) Personal learning planning: strategies for pupil learning, *Forum*, 43 (2): 67–9.

Bunting, C. (2000) The age of assessment, *Times Educational Supplement*. 20 October 2000, p. 1.

Busher, H. and Harris, A. with Wise, C. (2000) *Subject Leadership and School Improvement*. London: Paul Chapman.

Buzan, T. (1988) *Make the Most of Your Mind*. London: Pan Books.

Capra, F. (1983) *The Turning Point: Science, Society, and the Rising Culture*. New York: Bantam Books.

Capra, F. (1997). *The Web of Life: A New Synthesis of Mind and Matter*. London: HarperCollins.

Castells, M. (1996). *The Rise of the Network Society*, Vol. 1. Oxford: Blackwell.

Clarke, P. (2000) *Learning Schools: Learning Systems*. London: Cassell.

Clarke, S. (2001) *Unlocking Formative Assessment*. London: Hodder & Stoughton.

Claxton, G. (1999) *Wise Up: The Challenge of Lifelong Learning*. London: Bloomsbury.

Clay, M. (1993) *Reading Recovery: A Guidebook for Teachers in Training*. Auckland: Heinemann Education.

Cogan, J. J. and Derricott, R. (2000) *Citizenship for the 21st Century: An International Perspective on Education*. London: Kogan Page.

Cohen, B. and Thomas, E. B. (1984) The disciplinary climate of schools, *Journal of Educational Administration*, 22 (2): 113–34.

Coleman, P. (1998) *Parent, Student and Teacher Collaboration: The Power of Three*. Thousand Oaks, CA: Corwin and London: Paul Chapman.

Conger, J. A. (1997) How Generational Shifts Will Transform Organizational Life, in F. Hesselbein, M. Goldsmith and R. Beckhard (eds) *The Organization of the Future*. San Francisco: Jossey-Bass.

Costa, A. (1996) Prologue, in D. Hyerle (ed.) *Visual Tools for Constructing Knowledge*. Alexandria, VA: Association for Supervision and Curriculum Development.

Costa, A. and Kallick, B. (2000) *Activating and Engaging Habits of Mind*. Alexandria, VA: Association for Supervision and Curriculum Development.

Cousins, J. B. and Leithwood, K. (1993) Enhancing knowledge utilization as a strategy for school improvement, *Knowledge: Creation, Diffusion, Utilization*, 14 (3): 305–33.

Covey, S. (1989) *The Seven Habits of Highly Effective People: Powerful Lessons in Personal Change*. New York: Simon & Schuster.

Craft, A. (2000) *Continuing Professional Development: A Practical Guide for Teachers and Schools*. 2nd edition. London: RoutledgeFalmer.

Csikszentmihalyi, M. (1990) *Flow: The Psychology of Optimal Experience*. New York: Harper & Row.

Csikszentmihalyi, M. (1996) *Creativity: Flow and the Psychology of Discovery and Invention*. New York: HarperCollins.

Csikszentmihalyi, M. (1997) *Living Well: The Psychology of Everyday Life*. London: Weidenfeld & Nicholson.

Cuban, L. (1995) The myth of failed school reform, *Education Week*, 1 November.

Cuttance, P. (2001) *School Innovation: Pathway to the Knowledge Society*. Canberra, Australia: Department of Education, Training and Youth Affairs.

Dadds, M. (1995) *Passionate Enquiry and School Development: A Story about Teacher Action Research*. London: Falmer.

Dalin, P. with Rolff, H. G. (1993) *Changing the School Culture*. London: Cassell.

Dalin, P. and Rust, V. D. (1996) *Towards Schooling for the Twenty-First Century*. London: Cassell.

Darling-Hammond, L. (1997) *The Right to Learn: A Blueprint for Creating Schools that Work*. San Francisco: Jossey-Bass.

Darling-Hammond, L. (1999) Target time toward teachers, *Journal of Staff Development*, 20 (2): 31–6.

Dart, B. C., Burnett, P. C., Boulton-Lewis, G. M. *et al.* (1999) Classroom learning environments and students' approaches to learning, *Learning Environments Research*, 2: 137–56.

Davies, B. and Ellison, L. (1999). *Strategic Direction and Development of the School*. London: Routledge.

Day, C. (1999) *Developing Teachers: The Challenges of Lifelong Learning*. London: Falmer Press.

Day, C., Harris, A., Hadfield, M., Tolley, H. and Beresford, J. (2000) *Leading Schools in Times of Change*. Buckingham: Open University Press.

Delors, J., Al Mufti, I., Amagi, A., Carneiro, R., Chung, F., Geremek, B., Gorham, W., Kornhauser, A., Manley, M., Padrón Quero, M., Savané, M. A., Singh, K., Stavenhagen, R., Suhr, M. W. and Nanzhao, Z. (1996) *Learning: The Treasure Within - Report to UNESCO of the International Commission on Education for the Twenty-first Century*. Paris: UNESCO.

Dennison, B. and Kirk, R. (1990) *Do, Review, Learn and Apply: A Simple Guide to Experiential Learning*. Oxford: Blackwell.

DfEE (2001) *Learning and Teaching: A Strategy for Professional Development*. London: DfEE.

Diamond, M. (1988) *Enriching Heredity*. New York: Free Press.

Dick, F. (1992) *Winning*. Oxford: Abingdon Press.

Dimmock, C. (2000) *Designing the Learning-Centred School*. London: Falmer Press.

Doherty, J., MacBeath, J., Jardine, S., Smith, I., McCall, J. (2001) Do Schools Need Critical Friends?, in J. MacBeath and P. Mortimore (eds) *Improving School Effectiveness*. Buckingham: Open University Press.

Donahoe, T. (1993) Finding the way: structure, time, and culture in school improvement, *Phi Delta Kappan*, 75 (4): 298–305.

Donovan, M. S., Brandsford, J. and Pellegrino, J. (eds.) (1999) *How People Learn: Bringing Research and Practice*. National Academy Press: Washington, DC.

Drake, S. (1995) Connecting learning outcomes and integrated curriculum, *Orbit*, 26 (1): 28–32.

Dweck, C. (1986) Motivational processes affecting learning, *American Psychologist*, 42: 1040–8.

Earl, L. and Cousins, J. B. (1995) *Classroom Assessment: Changing the Face; Facing the Change*. Toronto: Ontario Public School Teachers' Federation.

Earl, L. and Katz, S. (2002) Leading Schools in a Data Rich World, in
K. Leithwood, P. Hallinger, K. S. Louis, G. Furman-Brown, P. Gronn,
B. Mulford and K. Riley (eds) *Second International Handbook of Educational
Leadership and Administration*. Dordrecht: Kluwer.

Earl, L. and Lee, L. (1998) *Evaluation of the Manitoba School Improvement Program*.
Toronto: Walter and Duncan Gordon Foundation.

Earl, L. and Lee, L. (2000) Learning, for a change: school improvement as
capacity building, *Improving Schools*, 3 (1): 30–8.

Edmonds, R. R. (1979) Effective schools for the urban poor, *Educational
Leadership*, 37 (1): 15–27.

Elkind, D. (1997) Schooling and Family in the Post Modern World, in
A. Hargreaves (ed.) *Rethinking Educational Change with Heart and Mind*.
Arlington, VA: ASCD.

Elmore, R. (1995) Structural reform in educational practice, *Educational
Researcher*, 24 (9): 23–6.

Evans, L. (1998) *Teacher Morale, Job Satisfaction and Motivation*. London: Paul
Chapman.

Evans, L. (1999) *Managing to Motivate: A Guide for School Leaders*. London: Cassell.

Fielding, M. (2001a) *Taking Education Really Seriously: Four Years' Hard Labour*.
London: RoutledgeFalmer.

Fielding, M. (2001b) Students as radical agents of change, *Journal of Educational
Change*, 2 (2): 123–41.

Fink, D. (1999) The attrition of change, *School Effectiveness and School Improvement*,
10 (3): 269–95.

Fink, D. (2000). *Good Schools/Real Schools: Why School Reform Doesn't Last*. New
York: Teachers College Press.

Fink, D. (2001) The Two Solitudes: Policy Makers and Policy Implementers, in
M. Fielding (ed.) *Taking Education Really Seriously: Four Years of Hard Labour*.
London: RoutledgeFalmer.

Fink, D. and Stoll, L. (1998). Educational Change: Easier Said Than Done, in
A. Hargreaves A. Lieberman, M. Fullan and D. Hopkins (1998) *International
Handbook of Educational Change*. Dordrecht, Netherlands: Kluwer Press.

Fletcher, C., Caron, M. and Williams, W. (1985) *Schools on Trial*. Milton Keynes:
Open University Press.

Fletcher, S. (2000) *Mentoring in Schools: A Handbook of Good Practice*. London:
Kogan Page.

Friedman, T. (2000) *The Lexus and the Olive Tree*. New York: Anchor Books.

Fullan, M. (1992) *What's Worth Fighting for in Headship*. Buckingham: Open
University Press. (First published in 1988 by Ontario Public School
Teachers' Federation.)

Fullan, M. (1993) *Change Forces: Probing the Depths of Educational Reform*. London:
Falmer Press.

Fullan, M. (1999) *Change Forces: The Sequel.* London: Falmer Press.

Fullan, M. (2001a) *The New Meaning of Educational Change*, 3rd edition. London: RoutledgeFalmer.

Fullan, M. (2001b) *Leading in a Culture of Change.* San Francisco: Jossey-Bass.

Fullan, M. and Hargreaves, A. (1992) *What's Worth Fighting for in Your School.* Buckingham: Open University Press. (First published in 1991 by Ontario Public School Teachers' Federation.)

Galloway, D., Rogers, C., Armstrong, D. and Leo, E. (1998) *Motivating the Difficult to Teach.* Harlow, Essex: Addison Wesley Longman.

Gardner, H. (1983) *Frames of Mind.* New York: Basic Books.

Gardner, H. (1991) *The Unschooled Mind: How Children Think and How Schools Teach.* New York: Basic Books.

Gardner, H. (1999a) *Intelligence Reframed: Multiple Intelligences for the 21st Century.* New York: Basic Books.

Gardner, H. (1999b) *The Disciplined Mind.* New York: Simon & Schuster.

Garmston, R. and Wellman, B. (1995) Adaptive schools in a quantum universe, *Educational Leadership*, 53 (2): 6–12.

Gick, M. L. and Holyoak, K. J. (1983) Schema induction and analogical transfer, *Cognitive Psychology*, 15 (1): 1–38.

Giddens, A. (1999) *Globalization: An Irresistible Force* quoted in DailyYomiuri (June 7), NewYork: Global Policy Forum, www.globalpolicy.org/globaliz/define/irresfrc.html.

Gipps, C. (1994) *Beyond Testing.* London: Falmer Press.

Gipps, C., McCallum, B. and Hargreaves, E. (2000) *What Makes a Good Primary School Teacher? Expert Classroom Strategies.* London: RoutledgeFalmer.

Glasser, W.W. (1997) A new look at school failure and school success, *Phi Delta Kappan*, 78 (8): 596–602.

Goleman, D. (1996) *Emotional Intelligence: Why it Can Matter More than IQ.* London: Bloomsbury.

Goleman, D. (1998) *Working with Emotional Intelligence.* London: Bloomsbury.

Gratton, L. (2000) *Living Strategy: Putting People at the Heart of Corporate Purpose.* London: Financial Times/Prentice-Hall.

Gray, J., Hopkins, D., Reynolds, D., Wilcox, B., Farrell, S. and Jesson, D. (1999) *Improving Schools: Performance and Potential.* Buckingham: Open University Press.

Greenfield, S. (1997) *The Human Brain: A Guided Tour.* London: Weidenfeld & Nicholson.

Greenleaf, R. (1977) *Servant Leadership: A Journey into the Nature of Legitimate Power and Greatness.* New York: Paulist Press.

Greenough, W. (1997) We can't focus just on ages zero to three, *APA Monitor*, 28 (19).

Greider, W. (1997) *One World, Ready or Not: The Manic Logic of Global Capitalism*. New York: Simon & Schuster.

Guskey, T. R. (1999) Apply time with wisdom, *Journal of Staff Development*, 20 (2): 10–15.

Guskey, T. (2000) *Evaluating Professional Development*. Thousand Oaks, CA: Corwin.

Handy, C. (1997) *The Hungry Spirit: Beyond Capitalism: A Quest for Purpose in the Modern World*. London: Hutchinson.

Hargreaves, A. (1994) *Changing Teachers, Changing Times: Teachers' Work and Culture in the Postmodern Age*. New York: Teachers College Press.

Hargreaves, A. (1998) The emotional politics of teaching and teacher development: with implications for educational leadership, *International Journal for Leadership in Education*, 1 (4): 316–36.

Hargreaves, A., Earl, L. and Ryan, J. (1996) *Schooling for Change: Reinventing Education for Early Adolescents*. London: Falmer Press.

Hargreaves, A. and Fink, D. (2000) The three dimensions of education reform, *Educational Leadership*, 57 (7): 30–4.

Hargreaves, A. and Fullan, M. (1998) *What's Worth Fighting for Out There*. Buckingham: Open University Press.

Hargreaves, A., Earl, L., Moore, S. and Manning, S. (2001) *Learning to Change: Beyond Subjects and Standards*. San Francisco: Jossey-Bass.

Hargreaves, D. (1984) *Improving Secondary Schools*. London: ILEA.

Hargreaves, D. (1999) The knowledge-creating school, *British Journal of Educational Studies*, 47 (2): 122–44.

Hargreaves, E., McCallum, B. and Gipps, C. (2000) Teacher Feedback Strategies in Primary Classrooms - New Evidence, in S. Askew (ed.) *Feedback for Learning*. London: Paul Chapman.

Harland, J., Kinder, K., Lord, P., Stott, A., Schagen, I., Hayes, J. with Cusworth, L., White, R. and Paola, R. (2000) *Arts Education in Secondary Schools: Effects and Effectiveness*. Slough, Berkshire: NFER.

Harris, A. (2001) Building the capacity for school improvement, *School Leadership and Management*, 21 (30): 261–70.

Harter, P. M. (2000) Earth's population, quoted in R. B. Bieler, *International News: Inclusion and Universal Cooperation*, www.disabilityworld.org/April-May 2000/IntntalNews/Inclusion.html

Hattie, J. (1999) Influences on student learning, *The International Principal*, 5 (30): 7–9.

Hill, P. W. and Crévola, C. A. (1997) *The Literacy Challenge in Australian Primary Schools*. IARTV Seminar Series No. 69. Melbourne: IARTV.

Hill, P. and Russell, V. J. (1999) Systemic, Whole-school Reform of the Middle Years of Schooling, in R. J. Bosker, B. P. M. Creemers and S. Stringfield (eds) *Enhancing Educational Excellence, Equity and Efficiency: Evidence from Evaluations of Systems and Schools in Change*. Dordrecht, Netherlands: Kluwer.

Hirsch, S. (2001) We're growing and changing, *Journal of Staff Development*, 22 (3): 10–17.

Hopkins, D. (2001a) *School Improvement for Real*. London: RoutledgeFalmer.

Hopkins, D. (2001b) *Improving the Quality of Education for All: The Theory and Practice of School Improvement*. London: David Fulton.

Hopkins, D., Ainscow, M. and West, M. (1994) *School Improvement in an Era of Change*. London: Cassell.

Huberman, M. (1988) Teachers' careers and school improvement, *Journal of Curriculum Studies*, 20 (2): 119–32.

Huberman, M. (1992) Critical Introduction, in M. G. Fullan, *Successful School Improvement*. Buckingham: Open University Press and Toronto: OISE Press.

Hutton, W. (1996). *The State We're In*. London: Vintage.

James, C. (2000) Personal correspondence.

Jaworski, J. (1998) *Synchronicity: The Inner Path of Leadership*. San Francisco: Berrett-Koehler.

Jensen, E. (1998) *Teaching With the Brain in Mind*. Alexandria, VA: Association for Supervision and Curriculum Development.

Johnson, D. W., Johnson, R., Holubec, E. J. and Roy, P. (1984) *Circles of Learning: Cooperation in the Classroom*. Alexandria, VA: ASCD.

Johnson, D. W., Maruyama, G., Johnson, R., Nelson, D. and Skon, L. (1982) Effects of co-operative, competitive and individualistic goal structures on achievement: a meta-analysis, *Psychological Bulletin*, 89 (1): 47–62.

Kerfoot, S. and Nethercott, G. (1999) The LEA and School Improvement, in G. Southworth and P. Lincoln (eds) *Supporting Improving Primary Schools: The Role of Heads and LEAs in Raising Standards*. London: Falmer Press.

Killion, J. (1999) Journaling, *Journal of Staff Development*, 20 (3): 36–7.

King, M. B. and Newmann, F. M. (2001) Building school capacity through professional development: conceptual and empirical considerations, *The International Journal of Educational Management*, 15 (2): 86–93.

Knowles, M. S. (1980) *The Modern Practice of Adult Education: From Pedagogy to Androgogy*. Chicago: Follett.

Kohn, A. (1996) *Beyond Discipline: From Compliance to Community*. Alexandria, VA: ASCD.

Kolb, D. (1984) *Experiential Learning: Experience as the Source of Learning and Development*. Englewood Cliffs, NJ: Prenctice-Hall.

Kouzes, J. M. and Posner, B. Z. (2000) The Janusian Leader, in S. Chowdhury (ed.) *Management 21C: New Visions for the New Millennium*. London: Financial Times/Prentice Hall.

Lafleur, C. (2001) *The Time of Our Lives: Learning from the Time Experiences of Teachers and Administrators During a Period of Educational Reform.* OISE/University of Toronto: Unpublished PhD thesis.

Lambert, N. M. and McCombs, B. L. (1998) *How Students Learn: Reforming Schools Through Learner-Centered Education.* Washington, DC: APA.

Lasch, C. (1995) *The Revolt of the Elites and the Betrayal of Democracy.* New York: W.W. Norton.

Lauder, H., Hughes, D., Watson, S., Waslander, S., Thrupp, M., Strathdee, R., Simiyu, I., Dupuis, A., McGlinn, J. and Hamlin, J. (1999) *Trading in Futures: Why Markets in Education Don't Work.* Buckingham: Open University Press.

Law, S. and Glover, D. (2000) *Educational Leadership and Learning: Practice, Policy and Research.* Buckingham: Open University Press.

Learmonth, J. (2000) *Inspection: What's in it for Schools?* London: RoutledgeFalmer.

Leithwood, K. and Louis, K. S. (1998) *Organizational Learning in Schools.* Lisse, Netherlands: Swets & Zeitlinger.

Leithwood, K., Jantzi, D. and Steinbach, R. (1998) Leadership and Other Conditions Which Foster Organizational Learning in Schools, in K. Leithwood and K. S. Louis (eds) *Organizational Learning in Schools.* Lisse, Netherlands: Swets & Zeitlinger.

Leithwood, K., Jantzi, D., and Steinbach, R. (1999) *Changing Leadership for Changing Times.* Buckingham: Open University Press.

Lerner, M. (1997) *The Politics of Meaning.* New York: Addison-Wesley.

Levitt, B. and March, J. G. (1988) Organisational learning, *Annual Review of Sociology*, 14: 319–40.

Lieberman, A. and Grolnick, M. (1996) Networks and reform in American education, *Teachers College Record*, 98 (1): 7–45.

Lieberman, A. and Wood, D. (2001) When Teachers Write: of Networks and Learning, in A. Lieberman and L. Miller (eds) *Teachers Caught in the Action: Professional Development that Matters.* New York: Teachers College Press.

Linn, M. and Songer, N. (1991) Cognitive and conceptual change in adolescence, *American Journal of Education*, August.

Lipton, L. and Wellman, B. with Humbard, C. (2001) *Mentoring Matters: A Practical Guide to Learning-Focused Relationships.* Sherman, CT: Mira Via. www.miravia.com

Little, J. W. (1990) The persistence of privacy: autonomy and initiative in teachers' professional relations, *Teachers College Record*, 91 (4): 509–36.

Little, J. W. (2001) Professional Development in Pursuit of School Reform, in A. Lieberman and L. Miller (eds) *Teachers Caught in the Action: Professional Development that Matters.* New York: Teachers College Press.

Louis, K. S. (1994) Beyond managed change, *School Effectiveness and School Improvement*, 5 (1): 2–24.

Louis, K. S. (1998) Reconnecting Knowledge Utilization and School Improvement, in A. Hargreaves, M. Fullan, A. Lieberman and D. Hopkins (eds) *International Handbook of Educational Change*. Leuven: Kluwer.

Louis, K. S. and Marks, H. (1998) Does professional community affect the classroom? Teachers' work and student experiences in restructured schools, *American Journal of Education*, 106 (40): 532–75.

Louis, K. S. and Miles, M. B. (1990) *Improving the Urban High School: What Works and Why*. New York: Teachers College Press.

Louis, K. S., Kruse, S. and Associates (1995) *Professionalism and Community: Perspectives on Reforming Urban Schools*. Thousand Oaks, CA: Corwin Press.

Louis, K. S., Seppannen, P., Smylie, M. A. and Jones, L. M. (2000) The Role of Unions as Leaders for School Change: an Analysis of the 'KEYS' Program in Two US States, in K. A. Riley and K. S. Louis (eds) *Leadership for Change and School Reform; International Perspectives*. London: RoutledgeFalmer.

Louis, K. S., Toole, J. and Hargreaves, A. (1999) Rethinking School Improvement, in K. S. Louis, J. Toole and A. Hargreaves (eds) *Handbook of Research in Education Administration*. New York: Longman.

Lucas, B. (2001) Creative Teaching, Teaching Creativity and Creative Learning, in B. Jeffrey, A. Craft and M. Liebling (eds) *Creativity in Education*. London: Continuum.

MacBeath, J. (1998a) 'I Didn't Know He Was Ill': The Role and Value of the Critical Friend, in L. Stoll and K. Myers (eds) *No Quick Fixes: Perspectives on Schools in Difficulty*. London: Falmer Press.

MacBeath, J. (1998b) *Effective School Leadership: Responding to Change*. London: Paul Chapman.

MacBeath, J. (1999) *Schools Must Speak for Themselves*. London: Routledge.

MacBeath, J. and Mortimore, P. (2001) *Improving School Effectiveness*. Buckingham: Open University Press.

MacBeath, J. and Myers, K. (1999) *Effective School Leaders: How to Evaluate and Improve Your Leadership Potential*. London: Financial Times/Prentice Hall.

MacBeath, J., Boyd, B., Rand, J. and Bell, S. (1996) *Schools Speak for Themselves: Towards a Framework for Self-Evaluation*. Glasgow: University of Strathclyde QIE Centre for National Union of Teachers.

MacBeath, J., Boyd, B., Rand, J. and Bell, S. (1998) *Schools Speak for Themselves*. London: National Union of Teachers.

MacBeath, J., Kirwan, T., Myers, K., McCall, J., Smith, I., McKay, E., with Sharpe, C., Bhabra, S., Weindling, D. and Pocklington, K. (2001) *The Impact of Study Support. A Report of a Longitudinal Study into the Impact of Participation in Out-of Hours Learning on the Academic Attainment, Attitudes and School Attendance of Secondary School Students*. DfEE Research Report RR 273. London: Her Majesty's Stationery Office.

MacBeath, J., Moos, L. and Riley, K. (1998) Time for a Change, in J. MacBeath (ed.) *Effective School Leadership: Responding to Change*. London: Paul Chapman.

MacBeath, J., Schratz, M., Meuret, D. and Jakobsen, L. (2000) *Self-Evaluation in European Schools: A Story of Change*. London: RoutledgeFalmer.

MacGilchrist, B., Myers, K. and Reed, J. (1997) *The Intelligent School*. London: Paul Chapman.

Maden, M. (2001) *Success Against the Odds – Five Years On*. London: RoutledgeFalmer.

Marton, F. (1975) On non-verbatim learning – 1: level of processing and level of outcome, *Scandinavian Journal of Psychology*, 16: 273–9.

McCall, J., Smith, I., Stoll, L., Thomas, S., Sammons, P., Smees, R., MacBeath, J., Boyd, B. and MacGilchrist, B. (2001) Views of Pupils, Parents and Teachers: Vital Indicators of Effectiveness and Improvement, in J. MacBeath and P. Mortimore (eds) *Improving School Effectiveness*. Buckingham: Open University Press.

McCluhan, M. (1964) *Understanding Media: The Extensions of Man*. New York: Macmillan.

McCrae, H. (1995) *The World in 2020 – Power, Culture and Prosperity: A Vision of the Future*. London: HarperCollins.

McFarlane, A. (1997) Where Are We and How Did We Get Here?, in A. McFarlane (ed.) *Information Technology and Authentic Learning: Realising the Potential of Computers in the Primary Classroom*. London: Routledge.

McGuinness, C. (1999) *From Thinking Skills to Thinking Classrooms: A Review and Evaluation of Approaches for Developing Pupils' Thinking*. DfEE Research Report No 115. London: Her Majesty's Stationery Office.

McLaughlin, M. (2001) Community counts, *Educational Leadership*, 58 (7): 14–18.

McLaughlin, M. and Talbert, J. (1993) *Contexts That Matter for Teaching and Learning*. Palo Alto, CA: Center for Research on the Context of Secondary School Teaching.

McNeil, F. (1999) *Brain Research and Learning – An Introduction*. SIN Research Matters No. 10. London: Institute of Education, School Improvement Network.

Medwell, J., Wray, D., Poulson, L. and Fox, R. (1998) *Effective Teachers of Literacy*. Final Report to the TTA. Exeter: University of Exeter School of Education.

Merriam, S. B. and Caffarella, R. S. (1999) *Learning in Adulthood: A Comprehensive Guide*. 2nd edition. San Francisco: Jossey Bass.

Metz, M. H. (1991) Real School: A Universal Drama Amid Disparate Experience, in D. E. Mitchell and M. E. Goetz (eds) *Education Politics for the New Century*. New York: Falmer Press.

Meyer, W. U. (1982) Indirect communications about perceived ability estimates, *Journal of Educational Psychology*, 74 (6): 888–97.

Mitchell, C. and Sackney, L. (1998) Learning About Organizational Learning, in K. Leithwood and K. S. Louis (eds) *Organizational Learning in Schools*. Lisse, Netherlands: Swets & Zeitlinger.

Mitchell, C. and Sackney, L. (2000) *Profound Improvement: Building Capacity for a Learning Community*. Lisse, Netherlands: Swets & Zeitlinger.

Moon, B., Butcher, J. and Bird, E. (2000) *Leading Professional Development in Education*. London: RoutledgeFalmer.

Morgan, G. (1997) *Images of Organization*. Thousand Oaks, CA and London: Sage.

Mortimore, P. (2001). Globalisation, effectiveness and improvement, *School Effectiveness and School Improvement*, 12 (2): 229–50.

Mortimore, P. and Whitty, G. (1997) *Can School Improvement Overcome the Effects of Disadvantage?* Viewpoint Series. London: Institute of Education.

Mortimore, P., Gopinathan, S., Leo, E., Myers, K., Sharpe, L., Stoll, L. and Mortimore, J. (2000) *The Culture of Change: Case Studies of Improving Schools in Singapore and London*. Bedford Way Paper. London: Institute of Education.

Mortimore, P., Sammons, P., Stoll, L., Lewis, D. and Ecob, R. (1988) *School Matters: The Junior Years*. (Reprinted in 1994 by Paul Chapman, London.)

Muschamp, Y., Stoll, L. and Nausheen, M. (2001) Learning in the Middle Years, in C. Day and D. van Veen (eds) *Educational Research in Europe Yearbook (2001)*. Leuven, Belgium: Garant.

Nash, R. (1973) *Classrooms Observed: The Teacher's Perception and Pupils' Performance*. London: Routledge & Kegan Paul.

National Advisory Committee on Creative and Cultural Education (NACCCE) (1999) *All Our Futures: Creativity, Culture and Education*. Sudbury, Suffolk: DfEE Publications.

National Commission on Education (1996) *Success Against the Odds: Effective Schools in Disadvantaged Areas*. London: Routledge.

NEA (National Education Association) (1996) *KEYS Training for Governance and Staff*. Washington, DC: Author.

NFER (National Foundation for Educational Research) (2000) *Playing for Success: An Evaluation of the First Year*. London: DfEE.

Nixon, J., Martin, J., McKeown, P. and Ranson, S. (1996) *Encouraging Learning: Towards a Theory of the Learning School*. Buckingham: Open University Press.

Norton, C. (2000) Today's children are likely to live shorter lives than their parents. *Independent*, 19 October, p. 1.

O'Connor, J. and McDermott, I. (1997) *The Art of Systems Thinking*. London: Thorsons.

Olsen, D. and Bruner, J. (1997) Folk Psychology and Folk Pedagogy, in D. Olsen and N. Torrance (eds) *Handbook of Human Development and Education*. Oxford: Blackwell.

Open Society Fund (1994) *Dear Unknown Friend: Children's Letters from Sarajevo.* New York: Open Society Fund.

O'Sullivan, F. and West-Burham, J. (1998) Building the Learning Leader for the Learning Organisation, in J. West-Burnham and F. O'Sullivan (eds) *Leadership and Professional Development in Schools: How to Promote Techniques for Effective Professional Learning.* London: Financial Times/Pitman Publishing.

Pearce, N. and Hallgarten, J. (2000) *Tomorrow's Citizens: Critical Debates in Citizenship and Education.* London: IPPR.

Perkins, D. (1992) *Smart Schools: From Training Memory to Educating Minds.* New York: Free Press.

Perkins, D. (1995) *Outsmarting IQ: The Emerging Science of Learnable Intelligence.* New York: Free Press.

Perkins, D. N. and Unger, C. (2000) Teaching and Learning for Understanding, in C. Reigeluth (ed.) *Instructional Design Theories and Models. Volume II.* Hillsdale, New Jersey: Lawrence Erlbaum.

Peters, T. (1999) *The Circle of Innovation: You Can't Shrink Your Way to Greatness.* New York: Vintage Books.

Peters, T. and Waterman, R. (1982) *Search for Excellence: Lessons from America's Best Run Companies.* New York: Harper & Row.

Peterson, K. D. (1999) Time use flows from school culture, *Journal of Staff Development*, 20 (2): 16–19.

Piaget, J. (1980) *Six Psychological Studies.* Brighton: Harvester.

Pilling, D. and Kellmer Pringle, M. (1978) *Controversial Issues in Child Development.* National Children's Bureau. London: Paul Elek.

Pollard, A. and Filer, A. (1999) *The Social World of Children's Learning.* London: Cassell.

Popham, J. (1999) Why standardised tests don't measure educational quality, *Educational Leadership*, 56 (6): 8–15.

Porter, J. (1999) *Reschooling and the Global Future: Politics, Economics and the British Experience.* Oxford: Symposium Books.

Posner, G., Strike, K., Hewson, P. and Gertzog, W. (1982) Accommodation of a scientific conception: towards a theory of conceptual change, *Science Education*, 66 (2): 211–27.

Postman, N. (1999) *Building a Bridge to the Eighteenth Century.* New York: Alfred A. Knopf.

Prawat, R. (1991) The value of ideas: the immersion approach to the development of thinkng, *Educational Researcher*, 20 (2): 3–10, 30.

Putnam, R. T. and Borko, H. (2000) What do new views of knowledge and thinking have to say about research on teacher learning, *Educational Researcher*, 29 (1): 4–15.

Reed, J. (2000) *Strategic Thinking in the Malawi School Support System Project.* Unpublished materials developed for Ministry of Education, Malawi.

Reed, J. and Stoll, L. (2000) Promoting Organisational Learning in Schools: The Role of Feedback, in S. Askew (ed.) *Feedback for Learning*. London: RoutledgeFalmer.

Rifkin, J. (2000) *The Age of Access: The New Culture of Hypercapitalism Where All of Life is a Paid-for Experience*. New York: Putnam.

Riley, K. (1998) *Whose School Is it Anyway?* London: Falmer Press.

Riley, K. A. and Louis, K. S. (2000) *Leadership for Change and School Reform*. London: RoutledgeFalmer.

Robertson, J. and Webber, C. (2000) Cross cultural leadership development, *International Journal of Leadership in Education*, 3 (4): 315–30.

Robertson, P. and Toal, D. (2001) Extending the Qualitative Framework: Lessons from Case Study Schools, in J. MacBeath and P. Mortimore (eds) *Improving School Effectiveness*. Buckingham: Open University Press.

Robinson, V. M. J. (1995) Organisational learning as organisational problem-solving, *Journal of the Australian Council for Educational Administration (Victoria)*, 1 (1): 63–77.`

Rogers, J. (2001) *Adults Learning*. 4th edition. Buckingham: Open University Press.

Rosenholtz, S. J. (1989) *Teachers' Workplace: The Social Organization of Schools*. New York: Teachers College Press.

Rosenthal, R. and Jacobson, L. (1968) *Pygmalion in the Classroom*. New York: Holt, Rinehart & Winston.

Rudduck, J. (1991) *Innovation and Change*. Milton Keynes: Open University Press.

Rudduck, J., Chaplain, R. and Wallace, G. (1996) *School Improvement: What Can Pupils Tell Us?* London: David Fulton.

Sachs, J. (2000) The activist professional, *Journal of Educational Change*, 1 (1): 77–95.

Sarason, S. (1990) *The Predictable Failure of Educational Reform*. San Francisco: Jossey-Bass.

Sarason, S. (1996) *Revisiting 'The Culture of the School and the Problem of Change'*. New York: Teachers College Press.

Saul, J. R. (1993) *Voltaire's Bastards: The Dictatorship of Reason in the West*. Harmondsworth: Penguin.

Saul, J. R. (1995) *The Unconscious Civilization*. Concord, Ontario: House of Anansi Press.

Schein, E. H. (1992) *Organizational Culture and Leadership*. 2nd edition. San Francisco: Jossey-Bass.

Schlechty, P. C. (2001) *Shaking up the School House: How to Support and Sustain Educational Innovation*. San Francisco: Jossey-Bass.

Schön, D. (1983) *The Reflective Practitioner: How Professionals Think in Action*. New York: Basic Books.

Schön, D. A. (1987) *Educating the Reflective Practitioner*. San Francisco: Jossey-Bass.

Secretan, L. (1996) *Reclaiming the Higher Ground: Creating Organizations that Inspire the Soul*. Toronto: Macmillan.

Seligman, M. P. (1975) *Learned Helplessness: On Depression, Development and Death*. San Francisco: Freeman.

Seltzer, K. and Bentley, T. (1999) *The Creative Age: Knowledge and Skills for the New Economy*. London: Demos.

Senge, P. M. (1990) *The Fifth Discipline: The Art and Practice of the Learning Organization*. London: Century Business.

Senge, P. (2000) *Schools That Learn*. New York: Doubleday and London: Nicholas Brealey.

Senge, P. M., Kleiner, A., Roberts, C., Ross, R. B. and Smith, B. J. (1994) *The Fifth Discipline Fieldbook: Strategies and Tools for Building a Learning Organization*. London: Nicholas Brealey.

Senge P., Kleiner, A., Roberts, C., Ross, R., Roth, G. and Smith B. (1999) *The Dance of Change*. New York: Doubleday.

Sergiovanni, T. (1992) *Moral Leadership*. San Francisco: Jossey-Bass.

Sergiovanni, T. (2000a) Changing change: toward a design and art, *Journal of Educational Change*, 1 (1): 57–75.

Sergiovanni, T. (2000b) *The Lifeworld of Leadership: Creating Culture, Community, and Personal Meaning in Our Schools*. San Francisco: Jossey-Bass.

Sikes, P. (1992) Imposed Change and the Experienced Teacher, in M. Fullan and A. Hargreaves (eds) *Teacher Development and Educational Change*. London: Falmer Press.

Silins, H. and Mulford, B. (2002) Leadership and School Results, in K. Leithwood, P. Hallinger, K. S. Louis, G. Furman-Brown, P. Gronn, B. Mulford and K. Riley (eds) *Second International Handbook of Educational Leadership and Administration*. Dordrecht: Kluwer.

Sizer, T. (1984) *Horace's Compromise: The Dilemma of the American High School*. Boston: Houghton Mifflin.

Smith, W. F. and Andrews, R. L. (1989) *Instructional Leadership: How Principals Make a Difference*. Alexandria, VA: Association for Supervision and Curriculum Development.

Smylie, M. (1995) Teacher Learning in the Workplace: Implications for School Reform, in T. R. Guskey and M. Huberman (eds) *Professional Development in Education: New Paradigms and Practices*. New York: Teachers College Press.

SOED (1992) *Using Ethos Indicators in Secondary School Self-Evaluation: Taking Account of the Views of Pupils, Parents and Teachers*. HM Inspectors of Schools. Edinburgh: HMSO.

Southworth, G. and Conner, C. (1999) *Managing Improving Primary Schools: Using Evidence-based Management and Leadership*. London: Falmer Press.

Southworth, G. and Lincoln, P. (1999) *Supporting Improving Primary Schools: The Role of Heads and LEAs in Raising Standards*. London: Falmer Press.

Sparks, K. and Cooper, C. L. (1997) Hours of work and health, *Journal of Organizational Psychology*.

Starratt, R. J. (1993) *The Drama of Leadership*. London: Falmer Press.

Sterling, S. (2001) *Sustainable Education: Revisioning Learning and Change*. Schumacher Briefing 6. Totnes, Devon: Green Books.

Stevenson, H. and Stigler, J. (1992) *The Learning Gap: Why Are Schools Failing and What We Can Learn from Japanese and Chinese Education?* New York: Summit Books.

Stiggins, R. (1991) Assessment literacy, *Phi Delta Kappan*, 72 (7): 534–9.

Stiggins, R. (1997) *Student-Centered Classroom Assessment*. 2nd edition. New York: Merrill.

Stokes, S. and Cuttance, P. (2001) Executive Summary, in P. Cuttance (ed.) *School Innovation: Pathway to the Knowledge Society*. Australia: Department of Education, Training and Youth Affairs.

Stoll, L. (1996) The Role of Partnerships and Networking in School Improvement, in M. Barber and R. Dann (eds) *Raising Educational Standards in the Inner Cities: Practical Initiatives in Action*. London: Cassell.

Stoll, L. (1999) Realising our potential: understanding and developing capacity for lasting improvement, *School Effectiveness and School Improvement*, 10 (4): 503–32.

Stoll, L. (2001) *How Good is Your Local School, Really?* Inaugural professorial lecture, Bath University, 24 May.

Stoll, L. and Fink, D. (1996) *Changing Our Schools: Linking School Effectiveness and School Improvement*. Buckingham: Open University Press.

Stoll, L. and Fink, D. (1998) The Cruising School: The Unidentified Ineffective School, in L. Stoll and K. Myers (eds) *No Quick Fixes: Perspectives on Schools in Difficulty*. London: RoutledgeFalmer.

Stoll, L. and Myers, K. (1998) *No Quick Fixes: Perspectives on Schools in Difficulty*. London: RoutledgeFalmer.

Stoll, L., Bolam, R. and Collarbone, P. (2002) Leading for Change: Building Capacity for Learning, in K. Leithwood, P. Hallinger, K. S. Louis, G. Furman-Brown, P. Gronn, B. Mulford and K. Riley (eds) *Second International Handbook of Educational Leadership and Administration*. Dordrecht: Kluwer.

Stoll, L., MacBeath, J., Smith, I. and Robertson, P. (2001) The Change Equation: Capacity for Improvement, in J. MacBeath and P. Mortimore (eds) *Improving School Effectiveness*. Buckingham: Open University Press.

Swaffield, S. and Dudley, P. (2002) *Assessment Literacy for Wise Decisions*. London: Association for Teachers and Lecturers.

Thomas, S., Smees, R., MacBeath, J., Robertson, P. and Boyd, B. (2000)

Valuing pupils' views in Scottish schools, *Educational Research and Evaluation*, 6 (4): 281–316.

Thrupp, M. (1999) *Schools Making a Difference: Let's Be Realistic!* Buckingham: Open University Press.

Tomlinson, C.A. (1999) *The Differentiated Classroom: Responding to the Needs of All Learners*. Alexandria, VA: ASCD.

Tye, B. B. (2000) *Hard Truths: Uncovering the Deep Structure of Schooling*. New York: Teachers College Press.

UNICEF (2000) *Child Poverty in Rich Nations: Innocenti Report Card 1*. Florence: UNICEF ICDC.

Vaill, P. B. (1989) *Managing as a Performing Art: New Ideas for a World of Chaotic Change*. San Francisco: Jossey-Bass.

Vaill, P. B. (1996) *Learning as a Way of Being: Strategies for Survival in a World of Permanent White Water*. San Francisco: Jossey-Bass.

van Velzen, W., Miles, M., Ekholm, M., Hameyer, U., Robin, D. (1985) *Making School Improvement Work*. Leuven, Belgium: Acco Publishers.

Van Wagenen, L. and Hibbard, K. M. (1998) Building teacher portfolios, *Educational Leadership*, 55 (5): 26–9.

Vygotsky, L. (1962) *Thought and Language*. New York: Wiley.

Vygotsky, L. S. (1978) *Mind in Society: The Development of the Higher Psychological Processes*. Cambridge, MA: Harvard University Press. (Originally published in 1930, New York, Oxford University Press.)

Watkins, C. and Wagner, P. (2000) *Improving School Behaviour*. London: Paul Chapman.

Watkins, C., Carnell, E., Lodge, C., Whalley, C. and Wagner, P. (2000) *Learning About Learning: Resources for Supporting Effective Learning*. London: RoutledgeFalmer.

Watkins, C. (2001) 'Learning about learning enhances performance', *Research Matters No. 13*, Institute of Education, London: National School Improvement Network.

Weatherley, C. (2000) *Leading the Learning School: Raising Standards of Achievement by Improving the Quality of Learning and Teaching*. Stafford: Network Educational Press.

Weinstein, R. S. (1998) Promoting Positive Expectations in Schooling, in N. M. Lambert and B. L. McCombs (eds) *How Students Learn: Reforming Schools Through Learner-Centered Education*. Washington, DC: American Psychological Association.

Wenger, E. (1998) *Communities of Practice: Learning, Meaning and Identity*. Cambridge: Cambridge University Press.

West, M., Jackson, D., Harris, A. and Hopkins, D. (2000) Learning Through Leadership, Leadership Through Learning: Leadership for Sustained

School Improvement, in K. A. Riley and K. S. Louis (eds) *Leadership for Change and School Reform: International Perspectives*. London: RoutledgeFalmer.

West-Burnham, J. (2000) Leadership for Learning: 'Re-engineering', in B. Moon, J. Butcher and E. Bird (eds) *Leading Professional Development in Education*. London: Open University Press.

West-Burnham, J. and O'Sullivan, F. (1998) *Leadership and Professional Development in Schools: How to Promote Techniques for Effective Professional Learning*. London: Financial Times/Pitman Publishing.

Whitmore, J. (1996) *Coaching for Performance*. 2nd edition. London: Nicholas Brealey.

Wikeley, F., Stoll, L., Lodge, C. and Brown, J. (2000) Effective School Improvement: The English Case Studies, in de Jong (ed.) *Effective School Improvement Programmes: A Description and Evaluation of ESI Programmes in Eight European Countries*. Groningen, Netherlands: GION.

Wlodkowski, R. J. (1999) *Enhancing Adult Motivation to Learn: A Comprehensive Guide for Teaching All Adults*. Revised edition. San Francisco: Jossey-Bass.

Wolfe, P. (2001) *Brain Matters: Translating Research into Classroom Practice*. Alexandria, VA: ASCD.

Wolfe, P. and Brandt, R. (1998) What do we know from brain research? *Educational Leadership*, 56 (3): 10.

Wragg, E. C. (1999) *An Introduction to Classroom Observation*. 2nd edition. London: Routledge.

Index